CHOOSING GREATNESS TO CHANGE YOUR LIFE

LYNN ALISON TROMBETTA

Published by Larksong Productions
A Division of Earthsong, Inc.
Tempe, AZ 85281
www.LynnTrombetta.com

Health Disclaimer: Please note that this book offers opinions and ideas for introspection and enjoyment only. Seek professional or medical advice wherever it might be deemed necessary concerning meditations, opinions and other matters discussed within these pages. The author and publisher disclaim any liability arising directly or indirectly from the use of the contents of this book.

Cover design: Bob Haddad
Cover illustration: kevron2001
Color photograph: Rick Cyge
First paperback Edition: December 2017
ISBN-13: 978-0-9744878-2-3

DEDICATION

For my sons, Aaron and Jason, my grandchildren, Jeremy and Jered, and for all people, young and old, who are trying to find themselves in this ever-changing world. I love you.

~ Lynn Alison Trombetta

Contents

Acknowledgements

Many thanks to the numerous published authors who have reinforced and contributed greatly to the way I think about life and the power of love.

I offer a special "Thank you" and expression of much gratitude to the late Dr. Wayne Dyer for his long-distance mentorship and encouragement throughout the years.

Additional thanks to my freelance clients for their faith in my ideas, thoughts and writing for their online presences on topics of wellness, spirituality, and the beauty of Nature over the past eight years.

INTRODUCTION

I spent several years living in a cottage on the banks of Oak Creek in Sedona, Arizona. The experience was both inspiring and isolating, and offered unanticipated opportunities to pause and choose my thoughts.

I believe that I became a calmer and more introspective version of myself in that quiet place. It was there, gazing into the creek, that the power of Choice became crystal-clear for me.

In the depths of the flowing waters just outside my door, I could clearly see the ways I had spent precious moments of my life thinking about "then" in the past or "when" in the future. I realized that what I was actually seeking was a better reality from which to operate the present, or "now" time of my life.

I learned that the better reality I longed for is the place within each of us where our "Oneness" dwells. It is here that we discover our connected-ness to all that is.

Surrounded by lush greenery, tall Sycamore trees, and a bounty of wildlife, I more deeply experienced the consciousness of Oneness. In quiet contemplation, I realized the power to choose the very best in thoughts, words and actions for myself and for others.

It became clear to me that Choice begins in one pivotal moment of focus on what I desire for myself.

Powerfully, Choice contains my very intention, my values and the possibility to change things for the better at any time. As I strive toward better, my values support my ability to choose.

Season upon season my mind imagined the journey of the water from high northern mountains to the plains in lower elevations as it passed before my door. I painted and photographed the surrounding beauty, soaking up the nourishing energy.

Gazing into the flowing waters, I often thought about the state of our planet and humanity. I wondered, 'Is this the best that we, as humans sharing a world, can do? What in our lives defines our greatness? And how do we aspire to better and achieve something grander?'

Then one day, Nature led me to share my thoughts about Choosing Greatness...

The ripples of one's actions travel far. Far beyond the day, the month, or the year, and possibly far beyond a lifetime, these ripples intersect with the lives of others. To be mindful of this in our days on this earth is perhaps the greatest gift we can hope to offer.

— Lynn Alison Trombetta

PART ONE

THINK

~ CHOOSING GREATNESS
AT EVERY TURN

THE CREEK AND "I"
- A BRILLIANT MOMENT OF AWARENESS

I stood near the steps that led down to the edge of the surging creek at the Sedona home where I lived, but dared not descend to the water below.

She had been a terrific thunderstorm and now, treading on the edges of her skirt, I found myself hypnotized by the energy that followed her like the wake of a ship:

Careening through the canyon, the force of both water and air was palpable and seductive, and the moment was highly charged with the energy of life.

I ignored the chill of the air and the sting of strands of my own hair blown hard against my face as the powerful energy of the creek's water created a wind force of its own.

This brilliant moment of awareness was surreal: I could not draw the air in deep enough, absorb enough of the charge, nor could I fill my eyes with the sight of the energy dancing in all directions enough to satisfy my soul.

1. THE RIVER

RECOGNIZING YOUR TRUE SELF AND INNER GUIDANCE

"The two most important days in your life are the day you are born and the day you find out why."   ~*Mark Twain*

Living on the banks of Oak Creek in Sedona, Arizona changed me in unanticipated ways. As wildlife increasingly encroached upon the cabin where we dwelled, I began to see how my own energy had changed.

I recognized that, like the deer, the bobcat, the hawk and the eagle, I am simply a part of all that "is" and I became fully connected to the life and the land.

Close your eyes for a moment and ask yourself, "Who am I?" There is no wrong answer to this timeless question. You may have asked it many times before.

As you listen quietly for your response, you will begin to understand the whisperings from your soul. Although your answer may have varied through your lifetime, you will discover that there is something that has remained constant, like a river within, no matter what your circumstances or desires.

This is because your mind is not who you are…a river runs

through it and connects you energetically to all that is. This river, like every other river and the creek outside my door, has times of calm, and times of rushing waters.

Being near the water's edge, I often pondered similarities between the flow of the creek and that of my own eternal river. I began to observe my energy, both in body and mind, while the seasons turned round.

As I deepened my lifelong feelings of kinship with Nature and observed life flourish along the banks of the creek, I marveled at the advantage our thinking human brain offers: We can choose so much of what fills our lives. In fact, we even have choice over what and how we think!

Your brain is a tremendous resource, and is a tool for changing your life for the better at any moment. This is what this book is about: Choosing Greatness in your moments on this planet. Connecting with the Greatness that is your "true self" and discovering the power to change your thinking, your life, and the lives of everyone you connect to: a quality of Greatness strong enough to benefit the entire world!

Are you ready to discover these brilliant moments of choosing Greatness for yourself?

Personal Integrity: The Roots of Choosing Greatness

Having the personal awareness and the courage to choose to do the right thing in any given circumstance, no matter what the consequence, is the definition of "integrity." This quality of awareness allows you to make consistent choices that either have a positive effect on the experience of others, or at least do not affect them in a negative way. In other words, integrity means consistently choosing Greatness.

This is not to say that these choices will be easy, because it seems as though operating from this kind of strength is not always the norm in today's world. Often "the end justifies the means," and many people make choices without thinking of how they impact others. By choosing Greatness you will stand out as the exception and your personal integrity, that is, your "greatness" will shine for others to see.

Being someone who is honest, with both yourself and others, and whom others can trust is one of the most valuable qualities you can possess. This is because the value of the trust that others have in you is immeasurable and can bring to you limitless opportunities and possibilities.

However, you can lose this valuable reputation in an instant if you do something to damage how others see you. Unfortunately, it can be easy to convince yourself that you have a perfectly valid reason why your anticipated result justifies an act of dishonesty or an action that takes you away from your integrity.

A final word on integrity; avoid those who are not trustworthy. If a person is dishonest in one area of his life, you can be sure that he will be dishonest in many areas of his life. Walking your path of Greatness requires a truthful evaluation and awareness of your friendships.

Choose Greatness: Surround yourself with people of integrity.

Toh Wah Nele – "The River's Journey"

While my husband, Rick and I slowed our pace to match the speed of life after moving creekside, we asked ourselves, "Is the creek the bed of stones where water flows? Or is the water itself the creek?"

The question was not a new one for us to ponder. Many years ago, Rick composed an engaging piece of guitar music to tell the story of water born from a high mountain glacier as it traverses the land, tumbling and growing until, as a river, it joins with the sea.

During a performance tour to Santa Barbara, California, where we performed as our guitar and flute duo, Meadowlark, we had the pleasure of dining with Louis and Daisy, a Navajo couple from the reservation at Ship Rock, New Mexico. After dinner, Rick played his guitar.

When he shared this newest original composition with the guests, he inquired as to the Navajo translation of the piece's name, "River's Journey."

Louis paused to think deeply, then asked, "For the River's Journey: are you in the river, or on the river, or are you the river?"

Wow! His question reflected an ancient way of thinking and the metaphor allowed a new perspective on our own life journey.

Through our time in the creekside cabin, observing the changes in the water's flow, we came to know the inner guidance we each possess in an even greater way.

We frequently caught brief glimpses of this ever-present guidance between the densely forested landscape of our lives, and we recognized our true selves as we began to know our answer to the question.

Ponder this for yourself: Are you IN the river, are you ON the river, or are YOU the river?

In the River: Are you in deep water, going nowhere? Are you fighting or flowing endlessly with the currents?

On the River: Is life carrying you along? Are you floating without direction, or hoping to put an oar into the water, get some control, and change directions?

YOU are the River: The River is strong, following internal guidance, creating its own way, whether by a path of least resistance or by moving boulders and sculpting mountainsides, flowing freely in a chosen direction.

2. Self-Awareness and the Ego

~Navigating Your "River"

Were you able to hear an answer when you asked the river question, or did your mind interrupt your process with its own agenda? It is common to experience some blockage or resistance as you ponder such ideas.

In your initial thoughts, you may believe "who" you are is not grand enough. You may try to search within for greater impressions. However, the simple answers that easily flow from still waters deep within you must be heard and trusted.

Do you understand the concept that you are the river; the river that flows through all that is? Recognize this and understand that your mind and the thousands of thoughts it creates in each day are not "you."

You are the greater energy that flows. Choose to honor this. You are the river running clear; you are the muddy river; you are the shallows and the deep. You are the river!

The task is to learn to observe your own thinking. You will

likely discover that your own thoughts create any limitations that you experience! That is, the idea that you might have difficulty with whatever project or endeavor you have before you is the product of thought. In addition, limiting thoughts have the power to produce limited results.

I have heard it said, "The very fact you see this as a problem, may be the problem." With this idea, can you begin to see that your mind, and the thoughts you use your mind to produce, is the root of all your suffering and frustration?

When you understand that the mind is an amazing tool that you possess, you can more easily take responsibility for your thoughts. This tool, your mind, allows you to function and process the sensory input you receive from your world.

Colors, shapes and experiences would not exist in your reality without your magnificent mind to convert it all into meaningful information for you.

However, understand that the incoming information from this world is so varied and abundant that your mind loves to create shortcuts. This private language that is developed in each of us acts as "shorthand," or abbreviated stories, that connect experiences with emotions to assist in faster processing of all of this information.

When you were young, all things were new. It was as if your mind gathered and stored input on a 'blank slate.' Through time, you grew and learned. Your mind continued to connect things, experiences, and emotions to help define the world around you.

That is, your mind began to attach abbreviated stories to experiences, emotions and events that happened at the same time. Soon, because of these "stories," unconscious, unexpected responses could arise when you later encounterd a situation similar to the original event.

As an adult, if you blindly trust your immediate reaction to situations, the old stories and their attached emotions can occasionally mislead you.

In other words, responding automatically, without questioning your reaction or emotion can lead you to decisions not based on the reality, or the facts, of the current situation.

If you accept your early impressions of the world unexamined and unquestioned and make decisions based around those beliefs and the emotions they carry, it is as if you are entrusting a five year old, or a seven year old, or any earlier aged version of yourself with decisions you need to make daily in your life.

Therefore, it is important to understand how your own mind works. Developing the skill of taking a step back before you react, to observe each present situation you find yourself in, can often reveal much clearer paths for making your decisions.

Personally, I believe this "shorthand" is why so many in my generation struggle a bit these days. We developed our impressions of how the world works during the years leading up to the 1980's, a time of economic expansion. It seemed the world, nature, and our lives would always be in a pattern of growth.

We attained adulthood and it seemed that if we worked hard, it produced results. As a very general statement, in the United States the economy and our buying power was growing, real estate was booming, and our children were thriving. Our minds created a cozy state of comfort based on this paradigm. For many, the shorthand we created in our minds dulled our senses to pitfalls that might lie ahead.

As with all things, there is a cycle of rise and then decay. We reacted to changing conditions with our original, "automatic responses" and an internal belief that there would always be more. We soon discovered we had not taken time to develop skills of saving any of the fruits of our labor for the inevitable winter. Worse, in some cases, we had not developed the skill necessary to look past the mind's automatic response and see the reality of our situation.

That is, many of us had not learned to question our own

perceptions and were caught unprepared for a world that had changed all around us.

With this example, are you able to understand why your biggest roadblocks to creating the world you desire can be the product of your own thinking?

These roadblocks generally fall into two categories:
- Beliefs that self-sabotage
- Behaviors based on those beliefs that self-sabotage.

What is the difference?

Beliefs that Self-Sabotage

Beliefs that self-sabotage often grow from childhood experiences and input from parents and others. These beliefs were scribed onto the blank slate of your youthful mind. As you grew up, these ideas, rules and opinions of the world were generally accepted as truths.

For example, a man might forever fear dogs because one ferociously barked at him when he was a small child. From that experience, if he formed a belief that dogs are to be feared, he might unconsciously carry that fear into adulthood.

As in this case, without questioning why you fear, dislike, or are drawn to something, you are allowing the emotional mind of the child you once were to influence how you might react much later as an adult.

Behaviors Based on Beliefs that Self-Sabotage

Behaviors based on beliefs may become unconscious, automatic behaviors that self-sabotage your life.

Using the example of the barking dog once more, if the man's unexamined fear of dogs causes him to cross the street at the sight of one, even if it is a Chihuahua, then you can see how a belief is affecting his behavior.

Even more damaging are beliefs you may harbor which result in anger, frustration or prejudice that leaks out in your speech or behaviors and affects how you communicate with others.

The roots of self-sabotaging behaviors are as varied as our personalities and can stem from beliefs of unworthiness, anger over the past, the need to feel love, fear of failure and more.

Try this: Think of something you believe to be true about yourself. Now, think back to see if you can find the time and the incident that first caused you to think that thought about yourself.

Did you label yourself as "not good enough" or "not smart enough" or "not brave enough" or any other description that makes you feel less than the person you really are? Like the man who became afraid of dogs, have you held an idea about yourself that has formed the way you think and act?

Ask yourself now, "Is it really true?" If not, is it just a thought you decided to believe a long time ago which has affected your life in so many ways?

In spite of the original incident or experience, through examining your beliefs to discover whether this long-held impression is true, you can change and ultimately eliminate beliefs and behaviors that no longer serve you as the person you are today.

By asking yourself, "Is it true?" you put one foot on the path toward choosing Greatness. This is because a simple moment of pause to question the situation, before you act, allows you to choose your next response.

As you learn to pause and begin to develop skills in observing yourself, the source of beliefs that self-sabotage and behaviors based on those beliefs can be recognized early as the thought pattern from which they are born.

When it comes to problems, your pause will often allow you to "see it coming" and avoid actually going through the unpleasant experience in real time. Giving yourself the briefest moment to "Stop and Think" creates the space from where you can consciously choose what is best.

Most important, your pause will allow you to separate your thinking from the input of your ego and choose a response as the person you are now. That nanosecond of conscious consideration will help you avoid the influence of random thoughts and behaviors based on past situations, conditions or experiences.

Becoming mindful will "turn on the lights" for you. As you realize how connected your thoughts and actions are, it becomes easier to recognize how the random uncontrolled chatter inside your mind may be sabotaging not only your thinking, but your relationships with the world around you as well.

This quality of self-awareness reminds you that you are constantly in communication with yourself and the world.

Your Energy Speaks

Developing the self-awareness to keep you "in-touch" with what you are saying, both to yourself and to others through your actions, energy and body language requires that you stop and mindfully observe yourself at various intervals throughout the day. The effect of mindful self-observation will be as if you were to walk in front of a mirror or a storefront window and catch a glimpse of yourself:

How are you carrying yourself? What does your stride communicate? Do you seem confident or downtrodden?

Next, notice what your thoughts are at this very moment of observation. Are you more negative than positive? Is this quality of energy reflected in your posture? Do you notice tension being stored in the body? Does the tension show in the way you stand, the look on your face?

Observing and recognizing what you are communicating with your energy makes it much easier to shift your thinking into a higher place and lift your entire being up into a greater experience of life. The simple act of taking a moment of awareness to notice your "self" is all it takes to begin.

In that moment of awareness, you can consciously choose

what your next action will be. Your energy will change along with your thinking, and this change will be reflected in all you do and say.

Even at those times when a cloud of darkness enters your thinking, it is possible to recognize it as it develops and remind yourself that moods are simply fluctuations in the quality of your thoughts and feelings. Everyone experiences these fluctuations. Instead of falling into old automatic thought patterns and behavior, it is possible to focus on who you are, deep inside, and begin to operate from there.

Focusing in this manner as you strive for clarity and Greatness allows you the space to experience mood fluctuations without judging yourself.

More importantly, you will develop the strength to choose your response to the ebb and flow of emotion without giving in to any negative tide which you know will pass.

Therefore, as you remove the layers of who you "are not," a subtle understanding grows within and brings more clarity for who you "are."

This brings us back to the river…

Although the creek outside my door flowed day and night, there were areas of it that settled into cool, mossy ponds along the way. The mind has similar places of repose; dark, deep, quiet spots filled with mystery waiting to be explored. It is within quiet spots such as these, in meditation, where my ideas of choosing Greatness became crystal-clear. Like a favorite swimming hole, it is enticing to slip into the water and enjoy the sensations of freedom.

Aah, now this is where I want to be!

3. MANIFESTING A BETTER LIFE FOR ALL

BY CHOOSING GREATNESS FOR YOURSELF

Like the river, we are each constantly in flux. Our hopes and dreams, our moods and desires swirl about, begging for attention.

How does one focus and become aware of a true desire, a dream that benefits the planet, not just one person, and is so right with the universe it has a power of its own?

We have all heard much advice over manifesting good in our lives. Some believe that tools such as Dream Boards and positive affirmations can lead the way. However, what are the true mechanics of this?

You may be wondering, "What if I no longer know what I want? What if I feel lost and I have never really known?"

I have heard my own mind speak in a steady progression of desires that lead me forward: 'I want. I want something. I want something different. I want something better.'

As you can see, at first, this "want" seemed somewhat

vague, and while others expressed desires for "things," I often found myself longing for energy and synergy to utilize for changing my life. At times, the secret behind attaining greater vitality seemed to be behind a door I could not pry open. It felt entirely out of reach.

However, through time and experience I grew, I changed. I began to experience an even greater connection to the world around me. A desire grew inside of me; 'I want to do something that has value for the world. I want that value to fill me with energy and passion.'

And grew; 'I want the energy of that value to create more value. I want it to sustain me so my artistic force gives back to others and to myself. I want that value to transcend my lifetime!'

Fortunately, I discovered that choosing Greatness is the "key" that can unlock the door.

The act of choosing Greatness recognizes our connection to others, our "Oneness," in ordinary moments. This awareness allows changes to occur naturally. Being open and receptive helps our desires grow to fruition.

For you, this openness together with the singular commitment to pause and choose Greatness honors your connection to your world. Your conscious pause brings awareness of the situation and choosing Greatness helps to remove any doubt about which path to choose.

When you view everything as a choice and an opportunity to learn and develop, grow and improve, you become "in flow" with the cycles of life.

You begin to better know a part of you, your higher self that will act as an internal guidance system throughout your life. The choice of willingness to receive health, happiness and success creates fertile ground for this growth.

More About "Oneness"

Imagine an ocean of energy.

Imagine that miraculously this ocean contains everything that ever was, and ever will be. The energy within this ocean flows through and connects the energy of everything that exists here.

Floating in this energy, you could also imagine, and quite possibly "feel" a connection to everything in this oceanic world. You would have awareness that there is no separation between you and everything else in this world.

Twentieth-century science has arrived at just such a conclusion regarding our universe: There evidently is no separation between you and other living things on this planet. There is no separation between the energy of you and the One underlying energy that is within you, surrounds you, and connects you to everything in the universe.

Our science is relatively new, but this idea of "Oneness" is ancient. Teachers throughout the ages have maintained that we are constantly communicating with everything in our world, and our world is communicating with us.

Additionally, it is easy for us to accept wireless communication as we use our cellular phones and devices. Apply this same ease of acceptance to the idea that we, as living beings on this planet, have the ability to receive and transmit messages within our world.

This receiving takes a quality of awareness that you can develop over time. The key is to quiet your mind enough to allow this to occur. The more quiet your mind, the more powerfully you will "tune in" to communication between your own body, your mind and your environment. Meditation can help.

It may seem that we are focusing on a 'quiet mind' and the experience of Oneness as 'inner' events. However, being able to attain a quiet mind and experience Oneness will allow you access to incredibly powerful ways of choosing Greatness in your everyday life. That is, with an awareness of Oneness, you can see more clearly, assess situations more accurately and sense what to do when you need to take action.

The Choice

One small step at a time, move closer to the continuous connection of Oneness. Begin to use awareness of your Oneness to communicate and work with everything in your experience as if it is a part of yourself, because it is.

Your increasing awareness of Oneness will help you to heal the places where you hurt. As you heal, you will naturally begin to radiate this beautiful connection to others around you. You will become more aware of your world. By choosing Greatness for yourself, you will choose Greatness for everything with which you come in contact and your energy will radiate out, creating good for others and the planet.

As you travel life's roads from a place of openness, you will naturally gain confidence and trust in your connection to Oneness. Allow this inseparable connection to be your guide. Finding and staying on the path becomes easier, which leads to your own Greatness as well as the collective Greatness of all humans.

The quality of your thinking will become passionate and joyful about the gift of life that you have received, and will encompass awareness and responsibility about the power of your mind. You will begin to see the world from a different perspective and challenge your thinking: Is this really the best we can do?

You will feel the "connectedness" to all that "is." You will truly understand that what you do to others and to our planet, you do to yourself. Thoughtful choices created in the moment from this place of Oneness reach for all the good that is possible within the hearts of humanity.

Furthermore, as you consciously allow feelings of happiness and success to flow into your life you begin to align with the same powerful forces that create Greatness in Nature.

You will begin to notice this energy in simple, everyday life. Enjoy and observe Nature's Greatness as she awakens sleeping plants and animals and spreads a patchwork of color across the land in the spring and summer, and then turns toward times of dormancy and quiet with the coming of fall and winter.

Be mindful. Be grateful. Be present, and choose this Greatness for yourself.

4. Three Kinds of Energy

Have you ever wondered where our energy comes from, what is its source? Flowing like the river, where does it begin?

On the other hand, is this something you have never given any thought?

It is easy to take our energy for granted until its flow diminishes and we are desperately seeking ways to bring it back.

I believe that choosing Greatness will allow your energy to return and your vitality for life to soar.

How brilliant might your energy be if you were naturally able to navigate life's challenges with a centered fitness that blooms from within? How great it would feel to trust yourself, knowing that at each opportunity you would automatically choose a better choice, a choice that adds a sterling quality to your life journey.

I believe this is within the vast realm of possibility. Can you also believe it?

Physical Energy

First, let's get physical: The external basic needs of your physical body are relatively few, being oxygen, water, food, and shelter. These basic elements will keep your physical body operating. However, life is so much more than this.

As you acknowledge that life can be complex and often beyond control, it is wise to look mindfully to Nature for the best clues on how to maximize the physical aspect of yourself.

See how the the animal world is alive with activity that exercises the body in search of food to nourish it. Observe the resting and waking cycles in Nature and understand that rest is necessary to recharge for the next cycle of activity.

With modern life, there are so many commitments to keep pace with and so much information flowing through daily life to address that it seems there is little time for needed cycles of inactivity. Additionally, your sleep may be affected and you may develop an ongoing general tiredness that drags down your productivity and zest for life.

If you add recreational drugs or alcohol into the mix, you have a recipe for damaging both your mind and your body.

You need your physical body to be part of this world, and you only get one.

You need your mind, for it is your greatest tool for survival.

The commitment to pause and choose Greatness will allow you to be gentle with yourself. You will begin to restore balance as you remind yourself that the natural cycles of life have periods of rest built in. It is a fact of Nature.

Through healthy activity, good food, rest and meditation you acknowledge the importance of putting something into the bank before you take something out.

From a recharged place, you will begin to see through the eyes of your soul instead of through the needs of your ego. From there you will begin to see paths that lead to the greater good for yourself and others.

You will have the presence of mind to begin to choose your greatest option.

Emotional and Mental Energy

Once again, I look to the creek for examples about the natural flow of energy in Nature. This is especially helpful when I seek to understand my own emotional and mental energy:

The energy of the creek flow is constantly present, and constantly changing. You could say that the consistent thing is that it is inconsistent!

Sometimes, the creek water flowed full and clear with migrating ducks floating along for the ride. At other times, the deer crossed easily, grazing on green grass sprouts in shallow water glistening in the sun. Summer's thunderstorms brought strong, deep flows of thick, muddy red waters. Winter's melting snow traveled from northern regions to float by in small glacier-like chunks.

These fluctuations always entertained me and I quickly learned to read the creek. By observing what small changes were developing in the water's flow outside my home, I discovered clues to the more significant changes that might be coming due to storms in higher elevations.

Not unlike the changing creek, your energy fluctuations can provide clues to your emotional and mental states. By actively observing yourself as you go through your days, you will notice fluctuations in your energy. Observing these changes will not only give insight into your present and immediate energy and emotional fluctuations, but will also allow you to notice patterns within your thinking and behavior.

It is here, when you take time to notice the quality of your energy, where you will develop greater skills in choosing and manifesting your Greatness.

Please take a moment now and think about what you have just read. As you develop the ability to pause and observe yourself in thoughts and behaviors, you will exercise your Greatness Muscle and grow stronger for choosing better paths for yourself. You will no longer be a puppet that does whatever your ego demands. You will feel connected and begin to choose actions, words and thoughts that align you with who you really are: your Soul.

Spiritual Energy

Authentic power comes from within; it is spiritual energy. Spiritual energy is Oneness. Engrained within your heart and mind is the deep-seated need to feel this connection, this Oneness.

When it comes to experiencing this type of energy, your spiritual energy requires a practice of allowing it to flow naturally, rather than having to do anything.

This is why the practice of meditation is so essential. Meditation in its simplest form is developing the skill of quieting the mind and allowing channels of this energy to be open and connect with the purest essence of life.

As you begin to experience this energy, the understanding of its universal power develops. You learn how the energy begins with our source, travels through us like a river into the world and returns to the source within us.

Through this energy connection and Oneness, you will understand how it can be true that when you choose Greatness for yourself, you choose Greatness for all.

In this time of expanding enlightenment and understanding, many on the planet are beginning to feel the pull for achieving this shared Greatness. We have been evolving toward this for all time. And, although it seems there is so much chaos and suffering in the world, the need to find ways of helping each other is being quickly awakened and will grow in our hearts.

You will experience this call to Greatness in your own way, differently than I do and even differently than those close to you.

This is the energy of Oneness. Soon, you will begin to understand how within each of us is the power to create a better world.

This power is authentic power. It comes from within and contains life force. It is your mission to use this power wisely and well within your lifetime.

The Challenge

This, then, is your challenge: to choose Greatness at every opportunity and contribute to the evolution of humankind. Acknowledge your Greatness and begin living it. When you open your heart to the natural goodness that resides within, you can transform yourself and your world. You can truly shine with this brilliant energy and be a part of a phenomenal change that is underway.

At birth, you were given a brain. Science has told us that our brains are underutilized. There is definitely room for expansion here, so let's get to it!

The rest of this book is for discovering that pivotal point of choice that leads to Greatness.

PART TWO

DO

~WHY AND HOW
TO
CHOOSE GREATNESS

Introduction
to Part Two

When it's time to choose, choose only one thing: choose Greatness.

This thought bears repeating: Choose only one thing: choose Greatness. Not a myriad of things, just Greatness at every turn, for Greatness begins with kindness and is ultimately love.

In this section, as we discuss how to choose Greatness in everyday situations, the place of a relaxed mind and body is your starting point.

Through a conscious relaxing of your body and mind, you will create a place of neutrality, a clean canvas.

This fertile ground will bear fruit.

As situations and desires arise, if obstacles appear, or opportunities present themselves, this place of neutrality will afford clear thinking, and easy decision-making.

You will literally "see" the path ahead. It will open up and there will be no question, no doubt, no wavering over which way to go.

Keep this idea in mind as we explore how to "Do" this.

A Concept of Nature: Enough to Go Around

Living close to Nature, I began to notice the natural balance of things and how, it seems, there is enough to go around.

This world is filled with the interplay between her creatures, and creekside I fully recognized that I was a part of that energy. I constantly marveled at the balance of life. Every season and every time of day brought new ways to observe the drama of nature.

One August, a tree frog took up residence on a ledge of our home near the chair where I sat under the trees. His tawny brown color matched the wooden ledge where he sunned himself each day, and he seemed as curious about me as I was about him. The trouble was, there were so many birds around, I was afraid he would become a quick snack, and I was enjoying his presence far too much to let that become his fate.

I bought an amphibian rock house for him and set it on the ledge. After a couple of days, he got the idea and sat inside, sheltered from the heat and the view of birds on branches in the surrounding trees. I enjoyed his company for weeks.

Then one day, he was gone. Sadly, I had to acknowledge the interplay of life and the possibility that he had become part of the food chain. At the very least, he was just another player in the transitory coming and goings of the creatures living there.

Several days later, we noticed signs of packrats and their stacked twigs in the space between the wooden steps outdoors. The groundskeeper suggested we set traps right away.

Even though the packrats had chewed through several hundred dollars' worth of wires in our car's engine the previous season, the trap idea was not appealing. Mother Nature handled it by calling in rattlesnakes and Sonoran whip snakes.

With the arrival of the snakes, new dramas played out near the creek. Every day was different:

Sleek and stealth, a small whip snake waited with the upper third of his body poised in mid-air, preparing to strike at a motionless lizard. The two faced off, frozen in time. Suddenly the lizard leapt out of harm's way and the game was over! However, with the hungry snakes nearby, soon all evidence of packrats disappeared.

Even the plants and trees got into the show as young deer stepped out of the shadows in the blue-grey light of early evening and balanced on their hind legs like ballerinas to pick small, yellow apples from the tree with their teeth.

Of course, as they chewed the decadent bounty from Nature like contented pasture cows, the doe kept a watchful eye for approaching coyotes. At the mere scent of danger, the "lookout" would sound the alarm by stamping her hoof against the ground to send the troupe galloping off, white tails bobbing into the woods for safe cover.

The creek was teeming with life. After dark, raccoons came to the muddy banks to teach their young how to capture crawdads. Then, with full, round bellies the kits stood on their hind legs to see into the windows where our agitated housecats watched from the sill inside.

To my delight, a brilliant red cardinal passed through each day and visited my birdfeeder, calling loudly until I responded with more seeds. One day, as I made the conscious choice to watch his playful antics through the eyes of my soul, his calls brought other colored birds to the feeder! Suddenly, a dozen bits of life's glory in yellow, red, and blue filled the tree branches and entertained my soul's vision!

The Source of all is always talking! The biggest message I receive is twofold: Nature takes care of it all, and when we remain conscious of our connection, there really is enough to go around.

That is, there is enough to go around when we respect our individual place in the world. We will build on this idea as we go forward.

Understanding this concept will allow you to relax your grip on seeking "more" and settle into a basic trust of the universe.

As you learn to trust the universe, you will also develop skills in trusting your own internal guidance. Then, when faced with a choice, no matter how large or small the decision, you will trust yourself to choose the better option.

You can see how with enough turns toward "better" during the moment of choice, you will be continually advancing toward your individual Greatness.

5. THE BIGGEST CHOICE IS TO BECOME ENLIGHTENED

Yes, enlightenment is a choice. Just one of a myriad of choices life will bring your way, but this choice carries within it the potential to create a lifetime of Greatness.

Depending on your individual personal focus, you will find yourself choosing daily from options that affect every aspect of your life: your health, where you live, and how you live out your years.

Whether or not you are consciously aware of it, everything is a choice, chosen in the smallest glimmer of thought within the moments of our life. Moreover, it all adds up.

If, at this time, you are not living the life you would wish for, then pausing to reflect will allow you to see how your choices have led you here: choices made one moment at a time.

New choices made from a more conscious state of mind will produce very different results.

Your individual enlightenment depends on your willingness

to acknowledge the intimate connection you have to everything that exists in this world. From this 'higher' thinking you can realize the potential for not just your individual consciousness, but also for community harmony and global peace.

How do these changes happen? These changes are created through conscious choice, one thought at a time.

Through your Oneness with the pure energy consciousness that is your true nature, enlightenment is discovered. This is not something you have to attain or create. Enlightenment already exists within you.

However, it is something you must recognize and allow to be a greater driving force in your life. The only "doing" required here is to consciously choose it!

This enlightenment, the Greatness you will be choosing, is the manifestation of your true nature. Discovering your true nature will bring richness and meaning to your life.

Remember, even as you acknowledge the divine nature you are, the ego mind will interfere whenever it is given the opportunity. Yet, once you experience the pure essence of your true nature through practice and meditation, the choosing of enlightenment will become easier because you will now know what has been missing:

You will know what state of mind you are seeking, and you can find your way back home.

Our Natural Intention to Benefit Others

I believe that within each of us is a natural intention to benefit others. Yet the behavior of some in today's world would lead us to believe that this cannot be true.

In spite of the evidence to the contrary, I share with you the idea that when you have developed the ability to keep the ego's demands out of your way, a natural intention to respect and help others can be found within.

If we begin to understand the ways that Nature takes care

of itself on our planet, finding a path to shared goodness becomes more possible.

With believing that it is possible that Nature essentially provides enough for all, you can drop the ego's games of competition and jealousy and discover within yourself a basic trust and the intention to share and benefit others.

You will discover this natural intention to benefit others operates without condition or the expectation of receiving anything in return. Even when the "other" is someone you have never met, this goodness is inherent. It is a most beautiful aspect of your potential Greatness.

This is an important point to understand for choosing Greatness no matter what you do, or how you do it. By allowing your natural intention to help others be a guiding light, your Greatness will shine through. You simply must pause and allow a choice that is "win-win" for all to surface within your mind and your heart.

It is here, at the "trailhead," just where the path may diverge, where you will pause and choose your personal Greatness. More than just a fork in the road, the Greatness is always found along the higher path, the choice that benefits more than just you alone. It is the one path that clearly demonstrates higher vibration and higher awareness.

For example, I recall a discussion many years ago where a friend shared his thoughts on our responsibility toward the food we eat. As we stood at the edge of wind-chilled waters in Washington he said, "If I must kill to eat, then I would respectfully choose to eat a larger fish that would feed many, rather than many small fish that would feed only me. Meaning, one life, respectfully used for the benefit of many."

Thinking with this sort of broader perspective demonstrates the goal to choose consciously as you go through daily life.

Always consider that while your choice may move you along

your individual path, it can also contribute to the greater good of many. If you are reading this book, then it is likely that you have been blessed with much more prosperity and convenience in your life than a large population of earth's inhabitants. You have an opportunity and a responsibility to think more globally in your choices as you go through life.

By allowing this natural intention of goodness, which is an expression of your true self, to emerge you will discover valuable clues about your life's purpose.

When you remember to pause at the pivotal moment of choice, choosing the option that is an expression of your shining true self will seem the only way to go. Read that again:

Choosing the option that is an expression of your shining true self will seem the only way to go.

Doesn't this make choosing your Greatness a lot easier?

"Kind" - A good way to "be"

Have you ever met someone who literally seemed to light up the room with their presence when they entered? What do you suppose it was that drew your attention and the attention of others?

The answer is that you were sensing their energy field. Whether or not you are fully aware of it, your sub-conscious is constantly 'tuning in' to the energetic messages being sent by others.

Have you ever paused to think about the messages you are sending out to other people? Choosing Greatness concepts wrap around the foundational idea that the energy vibrations you receive and emit often originate within the realm of choice. That is, if, and when you are conscious of this interplay.

You are undoubtedly familiar with The Golden Rule, "Do unto others as you would have them do unto you." Some form of this sentiment is echoed in many religions and ethical traditions. As we understand it, the "others" referred to in the biblical rule, Matthew 7:12, encompasses all "others."

When you think of The Golden Rule, you may think of examples such as the giving of material things, acts of kindness, or avoiding actions that may cause harm toward others.

However, here I am referring to "kindness" which is chosen on an "energetic" level. Therefore, the idea of "kindness" may mean "a general respect" for others and care taken in our interactions with them.. This "Golden Rule" behavior is chosen as a value for yourself, without the expectation of receiving something in return.

Sadly, it seems some understanding about the "energetic quality" of our personal interactions has been lost in translation through the generations. Unfortunately, kindness doesn't always beget kindness in our world.

Certainly, you can easily sense when someone's energy is unkind, and if you are not paying attention, your returned response may mirror their unkind energy. It would make sense then, that through awareness the opposite could still be true: that kindness begets kindness.

The wonderful Maya Angelou once commented, "I've learned that people will forget what you said, people will forget what you did, but people will never forget how you made them feel."

"How you made them feel" is 'energy consciousness.' That is, the awareness of the pure energy behind the words and actions being shared from one being to another. This energy sharing happens countless numbers of times a day all over the planet.

With "compassion," another word for "kindness," you are able to sense, resonate and respond to the Oneness of our species.

Your energy truthfully conveys to others how you are feeling and who you are. Although you might sometimes use your words and actions to conceal your true feelings, your energy behind your actions will always reveal your inner reality.

This is why learning to choose Greatness is such an important ingredient for a happy, successful life.

Develop the mastery to generate kind energy and kind thoughts before you speak or act. Reserve judgement. Your message will be received and understood on a level of "energy-consciousness," and you will be participating in a pure and truthful communication.

You can discover new paths for your life through a genuine interest in others and a simple desire to leave a daily legacy of kindness. You may begin to see a need you can fill and discover new feelings of contentment and gratitude arise from deep inside as you respond.

Having the energy of kindness toward life will calm you and soften your personality. It will let you drop your feelings of competition, striving and scarcity and experience your connection to others.

Then one day, the light will begin to shine on what you need on the inside to feel complete. As you align your external successes with what you really want in life, your experience will become more meaningful and satisfying. This is true no matter how small the success may be.

With kindness, you can change your thoughts, words and actions. Compassion will help you change what you usually do to get what you believe you want. Furthermore, it will help you get to the root of what you really desire.

You will soon discover this ongoing kindness extends beyond performing small acts of kindness. It is something you are, not simply something you do.

Pause now to imagine it: feel what it is like to be this receptive, non-judgmental, warm energy. Let your heart radiate this feeling outward and experience the far-reaching potential of this 'kind energy.'

I challenge you now to demonstrate your Greatness: be

genuinely positive and share the energy of kindness at every opportunity throughout your day. It will change your life, one choice at a time.

Choosing Greatness Over Material Success

As you may imagine, when you let your feelings of scarcity, striving for material possessions and success dictate your choices, you alter who you are at your very core.

Based on the previous chapters, it is easy to see how moving the focus away from your "connected-ness" with others to thinking focused on gaining money or status will produce "disconnected" results. This is especially true if you are being unfair in the ways you go after these material things.

The critical element that comes into play is the quality of "intention" we have been discussing.

In fact, material success is more likely when you are operating "on purpose." That is, when your thoughts and actions align with who you are at your core, or authentic self. Actions born from creativity, not competition, will produce the material success you desire.

It should be easy then to understand that if you reverse the order of your thinking and attain material success at any cost, you may fail to achieve your true desire.

An intention that harms or cheats others weakens you and poisons the outcome by the choice you have made. An intention that does no harm and offers the best possible outcome given the variables allows the Greatness in you to shine.

You must first lay the foundation by acknowledging your true self, the part of you who wants to experience the comfort of the best outcome for all. Lay this solid foundation and the bricks you add later will align correctly and build, or create what you imagine.

Therefore, a critical element in material success and in life must be the quality of your intention.

Material success is a good thing that allows you ever-greater freedom in realizing the things you want to do, have and be. However, while doing a thing solely for the success or the money may work in the short term, eventually the voice of your true self will cry out for attention and remind you of your basic intention to benefit others and the planet as well as yourself.

From here, you can imagine that conscience is the brother of intention. For, although born from two individual states of thinking, intention and conscience will keep you on the path for choosing Greatness along the way.

Shedding Light on Your Conscience – A Helper at the Juncture of Choice

As just stated, a crucial element in your success at any endeavor will be the quality of your intention and your focus. Your conscience is an internal guidance system that helps keep your choices in balance with your true self.

Everybody has a conscience, although not everyone seems to pay attention to its messages. You have likely seen this idea illustrated in the cartoon depicting an angel on one shoulder and a devil on the other.

It is interesting that we do not usually think about our conscience until we have crossed a line with our action, word or thought. Then, just like in the cartoon, our conscious magically seems to make itself known. You know the feeling; you suddenly feel uncomfortable, unhappy, guilty and aware you are going against your conscience.

What if you, or someone you know does not seem to have a conscience?

It may be possible to be disconnected from that voice of guidance through habitual behavior and knee-jerk reactions. Rationalizing out-of-sync behavior is a common way of ignoring the uncomfortable signals from within and continuing with undesirable thoughts, words and actions. In this manner, "rationalization" is the choice that has been made. The results of rationalized choices only deepen the chasm between where you are and where you want to go.

A loss of connection with the conscience can also occur with the use of alcohol or recreational drugs, which serve to muffle or silence the conscience and disconnect us from our true self, allowing the ego to run rampant. Why disengage your powerful brain with substances that cloud your mind and muddy your judgement?

A good rule of thumb is this: If you need to justify a behavior, or convince yourself, then the action you are contemplating is probably moving you away from your true self.

The discomfort, the "inner voice" of warning, and the "heart felt" pause act as your own Divine call to awareness to help keep you on the right path. The challenge is to be aware of the change that has come over you in that moment.

How will you respond? This is a choice presenting itself – a chance for you to choose Greatness, and your conscience is standing by to help you recognize it!

If you go against your conscience, you are likely to suffer pangs of regret.

Conversely, going with your intuition and following your conscience strengthens you to your very core as your understanding of yourself grows and blooms, even in the face of adversity.

Above all, your conscience guides your will to stay truthful to yourself and perform right action, no matter the details of any given situation.

We all have a conscience. What makes us great is the individual choice to acknowledge its presence and follow its lead.

Nature provides enough to go around. Develop the skills to create what you desire, instead of compete for it. Your conscience will guide you in kind energy as you honor your Oneness.

Can you imagine how the world could be changed for the better if people began to use the guidance of their conscience to choose Greatness for the choices they make in everyday life?

With these ideas in mind we arrive at the starting point along our path: the decision to excel, your decision to choose Greatness.

6. MANAGING EMOTIONS FOR GREATNESS

What has blocked you from creating Greatness for yourself in the past?

Feelings of scarcity, jealousy and competition are just a few likely suspects that may have slowed your progress along the way.

How do you get control of the thoughts and emotions that have the potential to affect your judgment and decision-making?

Is it even possible to "control" your emotions?

When you think about it, your emotions are most likely to get out of control when you feel threatened in some way.

In their most primitive forms, emotions are the product of instincts that insure your survival: making sure you get enough food, that you have a safe warm place to sleep and are able to protect your loved ones.

Pretend for just a moment you are at a point of complete

emotional neutrality: Your body is relaxed and you have quieted your mind, creating a clean slate on which to mentally visualize an ideal world for yourself.

Can you see yourself as the master of your thoughts and emotions?

Just imagine calmly experiencing life's "ups and downs," navigating the stormy seas as easily as navigating calm waters.

Are you able to picture yourself with these two desirable states: neutrality and as the master of your thoughts and emotions?

Imagine you possess a presence of mind which is neither overly agitated nor passively absent, but perfectly balanced, right in the middle. From this vantage point, you are able to see the broad horizon well enough to choose your next move with clarity and presence.

How best can you achieve this state?

You must have the ability to become conscious of your state of mind at any given moment. This is accomplished not through self-monitoring in an obsessive way, but through awareness of what is happening in your body, not your mind.

This awareness allows you to notice any rising tension in your body. Then you can realize that the physical tension you experience is a response to a thought in your mind - a thought form of resistance, such as, "I don't like what's being said," or "I don't like where I have to be, or who I'm expected to spend time with."

Let's explore some ways to "catch yourself in the act."

What does resistance feel like for you?

Actually, you are used to feeling your resistance to Greatness. You know when you are not making progress on your ideas and plans. You can therefore recognize that when you procrastinate, it is born out of your resistance to things.

From here, you can begin to recognize the signs of your

resistance: You feel the negative pressure in your body. You notice the negative thoughts in your head.

As an example, take a moment to recall an uncomfortable experience or situation from the past. As you get in touch with the memory, ask yourself, "Where do I feel the discomfort? Is it in my body, my head, my stomach? Can I feel myself 'shutting down' to what is going on?"

Try to connect with what your thoughts were like, what your quality of thought was in that past moment.

Times of discomfort and the underlying resistance are revealed when there is discord between how you believe things should be and how they actually are in any particular moment. It seems these moments of discord go on presenting themselves, day after day.

Getting in touch in this manner, by noticing your signs of resistance to "what is," helps you learn about your body's signals for your attention in any given situation.

So ultimately, emotions are not meant to be controlled in the literal sense. Instead, our responses to our rising emotions are to be noticed and managed.

As you learn to acknowledge and recognize the messages your emotions are conveying, you will be developing a connection to your intuition and guidance from your conscience for how to respond and proceed.

What does non-resistance feel like?

So, just imagine for a moment, how it would feel to simply accept when "what is" falls short or differs from what you desire. Just accept things as they are in the moment and offer no resistance. Accept it all in the same manner that you accept gravity, or oxygen!

You may discover you are able to understand and practice non-resistance most effectively when you first become aware enough to notice your own resistance. Then, at that lucid moment, you can consciously let go and release the point of tension.

It is here where you can understand what non-resistance feels like: The blood flows warmly back in. The muscles relax and are free to perform tasks with ease. Your mind unlocks, becomes open and allows new ideas to flourish.

At Least "Get Neutral"

When it comes to your thoughts and emotions, it is important to remember that they have the power to hinder or help you along the way. This also holds true for the input, opinions and shared emotions of others. If you find that you are at a place where some confusion is working its way in, be quiet, be conscious and strive for a neutral state!

Once, when Rick and I were visiting friends in Los Angeles, California, the couple invited us to dine together in town. The restaurant's location required us to take two cars. Our friend insisted we should meet first and then take one car. He was adamant we would never be able to acquire parking for both cars at this popular eatery and we would be lucky to find a space for one vehicle.

I have always been good at manifesting parking spots, and told him so, but he continued to argue his point. I gently told him he was interfering with my positive thoughts and my confidence for finding two parking spots, and asked him to at least find a "neutral" state of mind. I explained that he was vibrating with all sorts of negative information that would push away any chance of our success.

He calmed himself and agreed to try. Fortunately, the universe came through and illustrated my point. By replacing his doubtful, negative energy with a balanced point of neutrality, we easily found two parking spots right near the restaurant's entrance.

Having the awareness to find a neutral position washes

away the emotion associated with how things may or may not work out and can open the door to an easier time of making your next choice.

How to choose non-resistance and find the point of neutrality:

1. Acknowledge the Possibility of Discord: This is the first step toward non-resistance.

2. Stay Neutral: While you accept the possibility of discord, be sure not to assume a negative slant on things. To prevent this, release the negative perspective and trade it for the point of complete neutrality. Give yourself permission to let go of the emotion and all of the ideas and fears surrounding the moment and achieve "neutrality."

3. Focus on what you want: From your neutral perspective, focus on what you desire. Staying neutral will guide you toward the path which most likely leads in the direction you want to go, and move you toward creating the Greatness you desire.

Remember to anticipate the possibility of discord, not in a way that looks for and creates the discord or difference of opinion, but rather in a way that acknowledges life will repeatedly offer this as a possible reality.

What comes of it when you offer no resistance from your vantage point of neutrality and simply choose your greatest option?

The answer is that the universe begins to guide you; you step into the river where life flows.

7. LOVE WORKS

ADOPT AN ATTITUDE OF SHARED GOODNESS AND GENEROSITY

Imagine Earth as a sort of Noah's Ark. As you develop your "sea legs," you will soon realize that, if we all respect and honor the planet and our fellow creatures, there is a balance to Nature. There is enough to go around.

Unfortunately, it is easy to be caught up in your own needs and wants and lose touch with what is happening around you. We humans do not always function with an attitude of shared goodness and generosity and consider what would be best for all.

Fully connecting with those with whom we share the ark requires a fundamental quality of awareness on our part.

Learning to see others as an extension of yourself and as a bit of the future of the planet where you live is the foundation for all that can follow in your thoughts and deeds.

Thus, a large part of choosing Greatness depends on your willingness, commitment and awareness, and of course, your own individual level of contentment.

The energy of love holds the key to fully connecting in this manner. Within this energy is contained all of the other positive energies we have discussed: kindness, compassion, generosity and more.

Holding the energy of love in your heart as you live the moments of your days on this planet can move mountains for you throughout your life. Carry this energy in your heart because it feels good. Hold this energy as an offering to others, as you expect nothing in return.

Just as harboring ill toward others can rebound on you, so will the energy of love return to you tenfold.

Choose love! Choose Greatness!

Where Happiness Begins

On the topic of love, it is important to understand that the energy of love we are discussing here is not limited to the idea of having a "couple's relationship."

Getting in touch with your dominating thoughts about your own personal happiness is an important ingredient for creating greater happiness for yourself and your community, with or without a partner. Simply being in touch with the feelings generated by these thoughts is a big first step in turning up the happiness in your life as you begin choosing Greatness.

At any time, whether you are single or in a relationship, the truth is you can pause to focus on your spiritual self and how best to love your life and love yourself as you are in this "now" moment.

While love is the key that unlocks doors to happiness, introspection and gratitude are the first steps toward loving relationships with yourself and others.

When it comes to happiness, where do you find yourself now?

Try this easy exercise:

Hold an Imaginary Ruler in your hands and pretend the left side of the ruler represents disappointment and discontentment, and the right side of the ruler represents extreme happiness and contentment with your life.

Where along this imaginary scale do your general, day-to-day feelings fall?

Now, try this:

Close your eyes and remember a time or place when you felt great happiness in the moment. Hold on to the feeling in your mind and experience all you can within the memory. Simply remember every sensory perception you can from that moment.

What sensations did you notice? Was the warmth of the sun on your face? Alternatively, was the air cool on your skin? Was there a breeze? Were you alone, or with someone? Could you smell fragrances or scents in the air? What sounds can you recall, either distant or nearby? What sights fill your memory of this time?

Were you smiling? Are you smiling now, as you call up the happy experience in your mind?

Recalling the high points, the "touch points" of your life when you have felt connected to the full, moment-to-moment experience of being alive can be a valuable tool for increasing your present moment happiness.

These high points and recalled moments carry a "soul charge." Taking time to allow yourself to focus on past positive experiences with gratitude is a gift of self-love that will recharge your battery and put you easily in touch with your true self.

Try the Imaginary Ruler experience again.

Now that you have reconnected with your "touch point" for a moment, close your eyes and visualize the ruler once more.

Where along the ruler's edge are you now?

Were you able to move your happiness quotient up the scale by recalling times of joy?

Stay in touch with yourself: how are you feeling now? Is the light of your soul connection shining through?

As souls, we are each inherently connected to all that is, to everything that exists. It is the recognition of this connection that deepens our spiritual relationship with life and intensifies the quality of our daily experience of loving life, loving others and loving ourselves.

As previously stated, simply being in touch with the *feelings* generated by your thoughts is a big first step in turning up the happiness in your life.

These feelings are the very place where happiness begins!

8. COMMUNICATION IS AN ACT OF LOVE

As you seek to discover and expand upon your own personal happiness, it is natural to want to share life's experiences with others.

Your personal integrity, charged with your values, has a major influence on your success in relationships with the world, with strangers, co-workers and loved ones.

Interacting with others requires skills that stem from how well you understand your own needs in tandem with a solid commitment to the "give and take" that is true communication between two people.

Being Heard: Giving Others What You Desire For Yourself

Have you ever been frustrated in a conversation where others dominated? Where it seemed that you could not "get a word in edgewise"?

We each have a deep desire to be heard, but conversations can often leave us feeling dissatisfied.

Yet, as powerful as that desire to be heard is, we often overlook the equal need in others. We crowd out their thoughts and valuable communications with our own private thoughts and interruptions and miss the opportunity to share in the energy that true communication can create.

From the time we were children we have been told to listen. Yet we spend a great deal of our energy and time during any interaction trying to be sure we get our point across. This approach overlooks the needs of the other and blocks the natural flow of energy.

It is important to look at the frustrating conversation from both sides of the experience. The sharing of ideas, which occurs in genuine communication, is an invaluable tool for building a bridge to the Oneness of all.

How do you listen?

Do you listen only with your ears? Listening involves your full attention, focus from your eyes and your ears, as well as your mind.

At the most basic level of understanding, communication seems to be a two way street: One person speaks while the other listens. However, at the root of it all, each of us wants to be heard. Being heard makes us feel empowered and valued and helps us to feel understood.

Just as important as whatever idea we are trying to express is knowing that the other person is trying to hear what we are saying. When we understand this desire to be heard as a fact about ourselves, we can understand what a gift it is to give this attention to the other person by listening attentively as we communicate.

It is helpful to step back and realize the best way for yourself to be understood is to try less to be heard, and to listen more.

If you are in a communication that does not seem to have an opening for your point of view, the tendency is often to push a little harder to get your own words in. Yet often, the more you push, the less likely that the other is listening, as they themselves struggle to be heard.

Pulling back a bit to center yourself and extend positive energy is a good way to assure your point of view is heard. When the other feels heard, it is likely you will be able to share your point of view. However, it is wise to recognize that there may be times when it is more important to just listen, and be content with not getting your turn.

By listening carefully, you will understand the other's foundation for the communication and will have an advantage for expressing your own views.

When you are mindful to exercise compassion in communication, you honor the other as well as yourself. Learning to relax and let go of the strong desire to be heard as you allow the conversation to flow naturally can draw better listeners to you and result in a more mutually satisfying exchange.

Here are some ways to share in conversations with others and add a positive spin on life:

Ask: A simple question such as, "What's new and good with you?" invites the other to share their "wins." News of a recent promotion, a new home, or a goal the other has met focuses on successes, no matter how small, and helps to keep the positive energy "vibes" circulating. People love a question that allows them to share a positive piece of their life or themselves with you.

Appreciate: Be bold enough to tell others how you see them and what it is about them that you appreciate. Keep the warmth in your relationships by acknowledging a great sense of humor, a kind heart, or whatever you truly admire about the other.

Be Aware: Keep an eye on body language as you engage in conversation. You do not have to study what various postures and hand gestures might offer because your mind is naturally able to pick up these subtle clues.

Again, you must be "listening." If you remain aware and are honest with yourself, you can detect when the other person has lost interest or become agitated by the direction of the conversation. Be perceptive and pause a moment to choose Greatness over ego in guiding the conversation back on track.

Be Receptive: Be open to the things significant people in your life can tell you about yourself. Trust yourself on the validity of their comments and use this feedback as information, rather than criticism.

That said, it is important to be aware as you engage in this type of communication. If the other is offering a supportive message, which rings true to your inner self, then feel free to accept the positive feedback.

However, if this communication from another does not ring true and causes discomfort in you, then allow yourself permission to evaluate the message and trust your own inner guidance. Do look for anything valuable that can be gleaned from their offering, but always trust yourself. After all, the goal here is to allow the good within you to expand and to share it with others.

Balance in the Middle

Foremost, granting the sort of attention that leaves space in a communication and allows the other to be heard and feel understood is giving others what you desire for yourself. Communication therefore seems to be more like a teeter totter… the participants taking turns, one person speaking, one listening and at times, both resting, balanced in the middle, connected in thought.

There is a moment of choice in every conversation where

you can pause to be fully present; to hear and clearly understand what is being said. Wait for it, and then choose your response.

Practicing good communication daily is choosing Greatness.

In addition, the good news is you have at least one more tool that will increase your power of communication ten-fold: Your intuition.

9. INTUITION: MESSAGES FROM WITHIN

The five senses of seeing, hearing, touching, smelling, and tasting help you to navigate your physical world. Your intuition, also known as the "sixth sense," is an internal tool of perception that guides you, especially when you learn to receive its messages.

In areas of communication with those around you, intuition can be an invaluable resource. This internal guidance system gives you "hunches" and additional perception in daily life.

For example, when someone is talking you may feel a vague discomfort or sensation that causes you to think that the truth is being withheld.

Alternatively, possibly without much thought, you decide to take a different way home and later learn that your decision helped you avoid a traffic jam on your usual route.

Additionally, information via your five senses also provides messages and helpful information to your brain. If you catch a falling object, reaching out without actually thinking first, you may have responded to unseen clues gathered by these senses.

These are both cases where intuition has come into play and alerted us to a situation through a visceral feeling or instinctive thoughts.

As you know, emotions can distort your perceptions of situations as well as your responses as you communicate with others.

Intuition can sharpen them.

To develop your intuition in communication, try an empathetic approach. You can exercise your intuition in conversations with others with these easy tips:

Focus: Remember to stop your own internal chatter and focus entirely on what the other person is trying to communicate. As always, listening goes a long way in communication. Listening carefully will reveal nuances and clues that would otherwise go unnoticed. In addition, your mind is able to process information from all of the senses at once. Therefore, while you are listening, you are picking up other valuable information contained within the communication.

Ask: Questions, which arise from your focused listening, demonstrate your quality of attention to the interaction. In a sharing conversation, asking questions can clarify the other person's meaning, and again, the answers may provide additional intuitive impressions. Questions reveal your focus and attention, but do remember to respect the other person's boundaries and privacy.

Listen: Try to listen between the lines. Listen with your heart and let your intuitive impressions of the person's conversational tone and body language have a "voice" that you can hear.

The simple practices above will improve both your intuition and your communication. If you have a feeling or intuition about the other person or the conversation, try to respect your impressions and honor the communication from that space, always in a spirit of compassion.

To develop your intuition for daily life, some of the same ideas for communication, especially the skill of focusing, apply. Throughout your life, if you have been paying attention, you have likely been able to intuitively "feel" when you are out of alignment with your soul and the greater good for all. This "internal guidance" rests quietly until you step off the path, then vague feelings of disquiet bubble up. The further you stray, the more present the feelings become.

Conversely, when you are participating in "right action," aligned with your soul, you know it. It illuminates your path and breathes vitality into the job at hand.

The skills of Focus, Ask, and Listen apply to listening to communications from your own intuition in the same ways as for communicating with others. In addition, remember, the gentle nudge of intuition is a powerful tool at the moment of choice.

10. YOUR PERSONAL BEST

If you are like me, throughout your life you have received messages from others to "do your best." Continually trying to achieve this goal can be stressful and frustrating.

The following quote from author, Don Miguel Ruiz rings true for me, especially where the output of energy is concerned.

"Your best is going to change from moment to moment; it will be different when you are healthy as opposed to sick. Under any circumstance, simply do your best and you will avoid self-judgment, self-abuse, and regret."

This idea is important to bear in mind and is at the top of my list of techniques for choosing Greatness.

When you carry the intent to simply do your personal best, with the understanding that your "best" may fluctuate, you can operate with a clear mind and an open heart. You have already anticipated the good which will come from your intention and the path is cleared for you to choose Greatness each step of the way. That is, you intend and offer your best to your chosen focus in each moment of choice.

This doesn't mean you are trying to be perfect, nor does it guarantee the outcome of your efforts. But it does provide a centered power to work with and the peace of mind that whatever the outcome, you will know your heart and mind were in a place of loving cooperation with the universe when you acted.

And as Ruiz points out in his statement, your "best" will fluctuate. If your health is something which holds you back, take heart in knowing you can still make the choice to do your best within the limits of your physical condition. If you struggle with emotional issues or depression, be gentle with yourself and easy with your choice and slow down to give yourself space where inner guidance can ease your way. If you feel overwhelmed or unusually stressed, by all means seek some counseling to help you through the rough spots.

The "best" that you will work with here is centered on steps which will lead to your eventual happiness, guided by your intuition. Your "best choice" will keep you on the path.

Beginning any task with the commitment of personal integrity to "do your best" puts the power of the universe behind your effort.

The Decision to Do Your Best

The decision to do your best is actually an easy choice, you just have to remember to pause and make that decision.

With this awareness you acknowledge who you are at your very core.

Exercising your Greatness Muscle frequently in small choices strengthens you in immeasurable ways which aid in choosing for bigger matters.

Through self-observation you will discover your tendencies in behavior, your automatic responses, your strengths and your weaknesses. With this kind of practice and loving self-discovery you will coax your greatest self out into the open and diminish those behaviors which do not serve you well.

It sounds too easy: You become great by choosing Greatness in the tiniest moments.

It is easy. Simply and consistently, choose the option that lights up your intuition and your heart.

Understand that you are a microcosm of the universe, made up of the same physical matter and functioning within the same energetic force. "Tune in," and listen with every cell of your being and come into alignment: Choose Greatness.

But, Don't Over Do It!

Doing your best is a great ideal to keep in mind. However, you must choose wisely over where to spend your energy. Be aware that directing your energy toward projects that hold little value for you, or holding too high of an expectation for doing your best can mean that always doing your best can become overwhelming.

My first year in Sedona and the year which led up to it were really tough. I had experienced a decline in overall health related to living in the Phoenix area. My mother later confessed to me that when I was a child the doctors had warned her that my pulmonary system could not handle the fine particulates in the desert air.

As I entered my fifties, the pollution had become an even greater issue due to all of the new freeways and the frequent ozone alerts in the area. This was not good news for a professional flutist.

Rick and I had known for years that we intended to move to Sedona. Things magically fell into place when a friend stumbled upon a cozy and affordable rental.

Oddly, after all of the years of wanting to be in Sedona, I wasn't having the anticipated change in quality of life I'd hoped for. I worked long hours, splitting my time between my online writing jobs and performing for tourists and selling our CDs to get the money we needed.

In fall, the Sycamore trees dropped their large leaves in the courtyard while we played our music, signaling that winter would soon arrive.

I was doing my best, every day. I had surrendered to being nearly robotic in my response to all of the change and the "doing" to manage it all.

Rick had found Sedona's music community and was working a good deal of the time. He grew concerned that I wasn't enjoying myself in the new locale. I was working online too much. For me, there was none of the rest and recuperation that we had planned. Soon it became evident that by doing my best, I was overdoing it.

The following spring, as I began to accept my current limitations, I discovered that I could still continue to do my best, but with a different mindset. I began to practice choosing what was truly in my best interest.

As my body and mind relaxed a bit, it was as if a veil was lifted from my eyes. My thinking became clearer. I instinctively knew that if I could "see" any situation clearly, I could change it for the better, no matter the time it might take.

This awakening grew as the weeks passed. I was able to let go of my fear about finances and understand that if I was meant to live in Sedona, it would work out. And if something different or better was on the horizon, it would all be a part of the journey.

The surrender and growing feelings of joy continued as I became more and more aware of my physical surroundings; the home, the raw beauty of nature and the good people who were filling up my life. My little choices began to add up, creating better health and stamina.

The truth I learned is that in spite of the pressure to overdo, we actually create our daily reality with pure intention, focus and of course, choice.

There is always a pivotal moment where you choose what to focus on and in which direction to allow your thoughts and actions to proceed.

Your choices become great by choosing Greatness in the tiniest moments.

You must simply develop the habit that changes everything – the habit to pause and choose your greatest option.

11. INSPIRATION FOR REVIEW AND RENEWAL

Creative Time for Yourself - It's All in the Mind!

I have loved to paint ever since childhood. As an adult, when my creative urge rises up from within I often hear my mind listing reasons why I can't respond: "I am too busy with other things. It's too early, or too late. We have guests coming later. I have work to do."

Whatever the excuse, it is easy to find a reason not to take time out for creativity and doing something I love.

Surprisingly, I have discovered that the amount of time that will be required to satisfy a creative urge isn't nearly as much as I might imagine. Here's a journal entry from creekside which illustrates my point:

2/1/11: Persistence of mind won and I took back some of my own personal time and went out to the studio. I began shortly before 2:00 p.m. and painted as long as it suited me. Bluebirds gathered on the branches outside the window, curious at my presence, and time stood still while I completely immersed myself in the joy of painting the view of the creek. I satisfied the creative need and surprisingly, I was back inside just over one hour later.

I am amazed at how much time I spend longing for the time to do art and how little time is actually needed!

Creative expression is a choice. When we deny those urges for color, spontaneity, and adventure we crush down a vital component of who we are as individuals. Other things happen as we work with our tools - inspiration and creative approaches to issues and relationships appear, and we discover new ideas and fresh ways of thinking. It is a worthwhile investment of time…we just need to give ourselves permission to come out and play!

Unlock Your Creative Power!

Creative Power is in each of us, yet there is a part of us that wants to deny that this power is easily within reach. When things don't turn out the way we thought we wanted, we block the energy and blame circumstances and others.

When you first read the subtitle, did you hear a voice inside of you say things that dismiss the creative person you are? Thoughts like "I'm not creative," or "That will never happen," quickly derail your creative urges.

This kind of blocking happens when you find yourself unable to fully commit to your dreams, even if you can't see how this 'failure to commit' creates the blockage which stunts your creativity. And by creativity, I mean the power which allows you to create not just music, or art, but the power that leads you moment to moment in inspired choices that literally create your personal world and affect the world around you as well.

Can you accept that every choice you have made in your life has led you to this moment? From this place of understanding, can you acknowledge that because of this truth, you have fashioned your life, your circumstances, even your world to be a certain way?

You create all of the time. Your thoughts and imaginings cause you to make the decisions you make and travel the roads you travel. These thoughts are always just a bit out ahead of you.

So, to become a better creator and get better outcomes, you need to develop better ways: first, to observe what you usually do, and second, to decide what you "want" to do, based on your deepest desires. This gets you off "auto-pilot" and allows your creative mind to spread its wings and fly!

12. "Where the Mind Goes ~ Energy Flows"

Many years ago, at a small bookstore in Santa Monica, California, a stranger interrupted my silent search and suggested a book from the shelf. That stranger was Allen M. Rosenthal. The book was his, *Your Mind the Magician* (DeVorss & Company).

In an illuminating paragraph from this helpful little handbook, he refers to the "Creative Mechanism," a term used by Maxwell Maltz, author of *Psycho-Cybernetics* (Simon & Schuster), to describe a computer-like guidance system we possess that guides us through the "doing-ness" of everything we attempt.

Rosenthal further describes the Creative Mechanism as "a magical garden hose" that is always 'on.' He suggests that by choosing, envisioning what you want, and directing the hose at it, you nourish your desires. Whatever receives the water – or energy – aimed toward it will grow and expand.

Thus, there is obvious value in being more conscious from

moment to moment of the images you have chosen as well as your expectations for outcomes.

Consciously point your attention at what you want.

You have probably heard the saying, "What you focus on expands." Conscious awareness of what you want can produce a quality of perception that detects opportunities and situations that are in alignment with your desires, as your very awareness allows you to respond.

Applying this simple concept of attention and focus on what you want, crowds out the thoughts that block your progress.

The truth of this can be imagined when you recognize how the opposite scenario of focusing on outcomes that you do not want creates those unwanted things and ruins your chances for changing things for the better.

It is such a simple idea: you can only truly move in the direction of your attention and focus. This is where choosing Greatness becomes so crucial: it is largely a matter of what you think about as you go about your day.

What is the springboard for your choices and your actions? You really do get what you think about, whether you want it or not!

The river of thoughts you are swimming in will determine from where you will make your choice to dive in. You require a place to begin where your desires match what is possible in any given situation. Your choice made consciously, rather than automatically, is a critical element in changing things for the better, moment by moment.

Manifesting with Words - A Reminder to Be Mindful

Your spoken word holds within the magic of creation. Born from your thoughts, the spoken word is a carrier pigeon for your deepest desires.

Have you ever said something unintentionally, and then regretted it afterward? You may have thought, "Where did

THAT come from?" But at the same moment, you may have recognized a familiar bit of a previous thought or belief hidden within your outburst of words.

This may also lead you to feel that you should learn to control your emotions or thoughts, but there is much to be learned from any message that has found its way to the surface and manifested in words.

Words are a powerful way of creating your reality. Understanding this becomes paramount to choosing Greatness. The task at hand is two-fold:

• Your beliefs and thoughts must match for you to speak your truth. If you are saying one thing and believing another, you will go nowhere and constantly wonder why you feel like you are stuck on a merry-go-round.

• You must remain conscious of your thoughts so that you place appropriate attention on the small daily choices you make which create your reality. From these choices, no matter how small, you will choose and create your personal Greatness.

Remember, we humans are a microcosm of the universe. We are made up of the same physical materials and function on the same energetic level as the universe.

Thoughts are energy.

Your words are energy, one step closer to manifesting your reality. Catch the thought before it leaves your lips and choose words consciously to help not harm, to create, rather than destroy. Use them as the tools they are to choose Greatness in the hours of your day.

Awareness Over Circles of Concern and Circles of Influence

Author Stephen R. Covey addressed the ideas of the "Circle of Concern" and the "Circle of Influence" in his book, *The Seven Habits of Highly Effective People* (Simon & Schuster).

His writings on how we design our lives with choices regarding happiness, sadness, success, failure, courage, fear, and even decisiveness dovetails with what we are discussing in *Choosing Greatness to Change Your Life*.

With his visual drawing of a circle nested within a circle, Dr. Covey illustrates the idea that challenges fall into the two areas which he calls our "Circle of Concern" and our "Circle of Influence."

Although you may worry or have concerns, some things are simply outside of your influence. This includes the actions and words of others and global problems, for example. Things that fall within your area of influence, that is, things that you can do something about, include the quality of attention you give your family, your health, how you treat others and your general attitude toward life.

It might be helpful to think of Dr. Covey's two circles as side-by-side and overlapping, rather than as nested one inside the other. This way, you can imagine an area of common ground in the middle. In many ways, this area may be the best place to focus your attention for change. Either way, it is important to be discriminating about where you focus your time and energy.

As you think about choosing Greatness in daily life, your mind may discount the idea of your possible influence over the reality you currently experience. For example, it is true that the weather is outside of your "Circle of Influence," even though it is within your "Circle of Concern."

The "choice" is to focus on areas where you can actually affect outcomes with your thoughts and actions. Those areas are likely to be where the two circles overlap.

After all, if you focus on situations where you have little or no influence, you are wasting valuable resources. Also, if you focus on things that are in your life but do not affect or concern you, for example, issues that belong to others, you are again squandering energy that could be used elsewhere to produce more value from your investment.

By training yourself to assess situations in this manner and mastering the skill of focusing your choices within your intentions, you will experience more positive outcomes in the general sense. Remember, every day brings new opportunities in nearly every moment and in nearly every situation to choose a different way of doing things.

Furthermore, you may never know the ways that a more holistic perspective and positive approach toward life has influenced things of which you might not generally be aware.

13. Gratitude and Abundance Go Hand in Hand

You've probably heard it before, but in order to create more of what you desire, you must first be grateful for where you are and what you have.

Does this seem easier said than done, especially if your feelings of discontentment are overriding all other thoughts? How can you experience gratitude if you are unhappy with the way things are?

Yet, how can you possibly change things by only focusing on all the things you do not want? And doesn't identifying what you do not want help you to recognize what you do desire?

Gratitude is the Key

Gratitude has the power to smooth the way and open a path toward your dreams. Feelings of gratitude experienced within let you understand the ways you can experience being "okay" right where you are in this moment. Gratitude means being thankful for all that is going well and releasing negative thoughts and emotions over that which is not going as hoped or planned.

Gratitude grants you an outlook which contains a positive, rather than negative vibration. Positive vibrations of any thought emitted by positive vibrations of your brain reveal your energy. The positive energy of gratitude will attract more positive experiences and circumstances to you.

While it may be somewhat difficult to imagine this truth, it is easy to see when an opposite, negative force is at work.

For myself, just believing the idea that we attract what we "send out" enables me to choose the better vibrational thoughts…even when life presents its challenges.

Gratitude can be practiced as you go about your day. After all, there is so much you have to be grateful for.

Being mindful with your gratitude over even the smallest gift you have received from life has the power to raise your vibration and bring more positive experiences and outcomes into your life.

We can conclude that gratitude may be one of the most vibrationally influential tools we have available to us to change our world, one thought at a time.

Introspection

Often, to experience gratitude takes some introspection, especially initially to jump start the feelings of appreciation. It is amazing when you realize all of the things you tend to take for granted! For a simple example, breathing and the oxygen that supports it.

I find when I allow my thoughts to begin at the point of an inhale and follow it through the exhale, not only do I remember my gratitude for the air, the moment and this life, but I am able to extend the feelings of gratitude until the warmth of Oneness envelopes my whole being and soon encircles the entire world!

Introspection leads us to the kind of gratitude which changes things. Spending time daily in quiet contemplation and introspection will allow you to explore the many ways you are grateful.

Introspection changes things because it changes your perspective. In fact, together with gratitude, it changes your perspective from one of looking out through the eyes of the ego, with all of its wants and desires, to looking out through the eyes of your soul with acceptance and appreciation.

Through introspection, you will discover that gratitude feels good! It will crowd out the nitty-gritty everyday "stuff" of life and bring a sparkle back into your eyes for all that is good in the world around you…because gratitude is a state of Greatness.

14. Meditation: The Bridge that Connects Us with the World

Imagine that through meditation you can create new circumstances for yourself, even create a "new" you. This is my meaning when I say meditation is the bridge that connects us to the world.

The world I refer to here is one of infinite possibilities, connected to our Oneness. This world can be experienced in your mind first, and then expanded with your creative energy.

Because meditation can awaken consciousness in your mind and heart and recover awareness of Oneness, contemplation or meditation for the sake of relaxation and peace of mind are only a fraction of the ways to use this powerful tool.

Through planting seeds in your mind, you commit to and create new outcomes and new realities for yourself. Thus, one of the most important uses for meditation is creation.

Imagining a New Reality

When you quiet your mind for meditation, you will soon discover that there is a state of mind available within you that is like a blank slate.

Try it: Close your eyes. The blank space you "see" might be described as "nothing," but it is actually your mind vibrating with endless potential. Creation comes from here and with conscious attention you can become the director of changes you would like to see manifest in your life.

Like a movie screen within the mind, on this space you may freely visualize the situations and experiences you would like to manifest.

During meditation, as you imagine what you want to create, strive to experience the object or situation with all five of your senses. How does it look, smell, feel, sound and even taste?

Experiencing your desire with the five senses, as if it already exists, is the "active ingredient" in the recipe for manifesting.

When you meditate, remind yourself that the good you currently experience in your life has come out of wanting it and then, on some level, making choices that led you here to today. Experience waves of gratitude for all that your life contains and acknowledge your willingness and worthiness for the changes you desire.

To assist you with this, Part Four of this book contains a variety of meditations for you to try.

15. RECIPE FOR MANIFESTING

Whenever we speak of manifesting, our imaginations dance with ideas of things and situations we would like to create in our lives. You may understand that through meditation you can develop skills of manifesting which lead to the fulfillment of those desires, or "fruition." But without understanding the process at work as you create energy toward manifesting your desires, your personal energy is likely to be scattered and your efforts may fall short.

Thoughts are the seeds we plant toward creating our tomorrows. However, a mere thought doesn't necessarily contain the quality of energy which brings about change. Pause to recognize energy fluctuations in yourself and truly choose your greatest option. Add emotion, passion or strong feelings to your thought and you have just watered the seeds!

The recipe for manifesting desired changes has yet another ingredient: As you water your seeds with strong emotion, your thoughts change from mere thoughts into experience. You are engaged in experiencing what it feels like to realize your desire. This is where visualization comes into play:

When you visualize an outcome and experience the strong feelings that being, doing, or having the desired object or outcome produces, then you have changed the energy one step closer to manifestation.

As you experience this change, remember to observe how you respond to your own feelings. By staying in alignment through this quality of attention on your thoughts and emotions, you are working with authentic power and are actively engaged in the process of realization and fulfillment of your dreams!

Some things seem easier to manifest than others. My husband and I still laugh about an incident which occurred some years ago. Here's the tale we call, "Manifesting and the Green Beans":

While enjoying a meal at a favorite restaurant, I was once again thinking about how much I love their green beans. In fact, I had the fleeting thought that I didn't want the green beans to end, even though I probably had more than enough already. Still, the thought continued to nag at me and teased that if I asked the universe for more green beans and received them, it would be a sign. Again, it was just a thought with only my affinity for the good flavor of the green beans attached.

In the next moment, Rick mentioned to the waitress that his side dishes needed to be reheated. She declared she would just bring fresh servings of potatoes and green beans.

I'd already forgotten the fleeting thoughts about asking for more, but it did register with me that if Rick was willing to share, I would have more green beans.

As the waitress returned and set Rick's new side dishes in front of him, she turned to me and said, "Oh, and I brought you more green beans too!"

And with that, I was suddenly surrounded by four servings of green beans...instant manifestation!

Of course, anyone I share this story with is likely to suggest that I move on to manifesting larger things!

More Food for Thought

You must always keep in mind the power of both thoughts and words for creating your reality.

Once, while visiting a gallery in Sedona, I observed as a successful sale transpired. An elderly couple and two friends were lusting over a beautiful Marble vase and a matched set of yellow Bumblebee Jasper earrings and pendant. Together with their friends, the couple pondered over the possible purchase of the vase. They clearly stated to each other how much they wanted it.

Separated from their friends, the wife tried on the jewelry and the couple candidly revisited the subject of the vase in private. Again, they agreed that they really wished to own the beautiful marble vase. However, the husband stated in equally decisive language that he did not want to have to carry it. He added that shipping the vase was too expensive and that he could imagine how difficult it would be to transport the heavy vase during their travels. He vetoed the purchase.

As the husband bought the pendant and earrings for his wife, the couple's friends purchased the vase at the other register.

The first couple suddenly became aware of the fact that their friends were engaged in the transaction. The wife looked puzzled. Her friend explained, "Were getting the vase...but it's for you as a thank you for all you've done for us this trip!" Then they added, "There's just one catch...You'll have to carry it home yourself."

This perfect illustration of manifestation served as a reminder to me that the messages we broadcast are clearly heard by the universe. With his spoken words, "I want the marble vase," and his visual thoughts about what it actually would be like to carry the vase home, the universe responded. Ultimately, the man left with the boxed vase in his arms.

We can suppose that with awareness, the best initial phrase would have been, "I want the vase if there's an effortless solution for getting it home."

However, I know that for myself, I don't always finish my own sentences and "out-loud thoughts" with such manifesting finesse, but since we are continually manifesting, it is food for thought!

How Thoughts Became Things: A Creekside Home

I would be remiss if I did not discuss Dream Boards as a final example on the idea of manifesting. I played with Dream Boards on a couple of occasions, without too much investment of time or thought. In fact, I felt as though allowing my subconscious a little freedom of expression might be a good plan as I played with the edges of dreams I held.

It wasn't until about a year after we had moved into the creekside home that I found my Dream Board among the stacks of artwork I had stored in a closet. This unassuming wood-framed piece of cork board and tiny, round pushpins held one small color clipping from a magazine that was nearly a photograph of the place we were living in: a small, redwood cabin facing the creek. It was if the photo had been taken from the opposite side of the creek, looking across at the home.

Furthermore, the other magazine clipping I had included on the board was a view of Cathedral rock from the opposite side of that which we could see from the home. Curiously, the positioning of the two photos was as if you were standing on the other side of Cathedral Rock, looking across the creek, toward the house!

In one upper corner, there was a small stamp-sized image of a snowflake that I hardly remembered placing there, and the day I rediscovered the Dream Board was our first day of snow at the cabin.

Lastly, I noted that the little photo of the cabin included some daffodils, my favorite flowers, at the front. I wondered how long it would take me to manifest a daffodil.

When spring arrived, the gardens on the property exploded with hundreds of blooming daffodils in all manner of sizes and colors!

Yes, the Creekside home was a truly magical place. A place that allowed me to reconnect with my Oneness. A place to dream and begin to understand how thoughts can become things.

So to review: Focused thought plus a quality of energy which contains emotion, passion or strong feelings leads to experiencing in your mind what actually realizing your desire would feel like.

This experiencing, also known as "visualizing," brings the fulfilment of your dream one step closer to physical reality. Because the dream seems so close you can feel it, your focused thoughts will begin to match the vibration of what you desire, and your choices followed with actions will begin to align with what it will take to create it for yourself.

16. Some Final Thoughts

Practice the Zen of seeing to pacify the left brain on the way to your secret garden. Then choose your Greatness.

We spend so much of our time in thought. Thoughts which come from "nowhere" and "everywhere" fill our head and tangle up, obscuring the clarity that resides just underneath the clutter.

When I truly learned to see the world around me, it was as if a veil had been lifted from my eyes. Suddenly, the artist awakened and opened her eyes. Colors were brighter, contrasts more pronounced and there was literally entertainment all around.

Where I had always felt the urge to paint things I saw in Nature, suddenly there was more surrounding me in every direction than could be isolated. More than could ever be painted. More than could be illustrated in a painting and certainly more than could be explained in words.

The glory is not fleeting, it is everywhere. There are miracles at every turn and more colors, life forms, shapes, energetic impulses and surprises than could ever be described.

Suddenly, the "need" to capture it, share it, talk about it or explain it abated. It was my secret garden! At 56 years of age, in the midst of the worst economy in my entire lifetime, surrounded by uncertainty, there was this solid, eternal place which is everywhere and nowhere, all at once.

I have become lost in it, entertained at every turn. Moreover, my left brain and its analytical processes as well as my ego's chattering have ceased. Both have become engrossed in the game of seeing, the "zen" of seeing all that was always there.

Like others, I had read about techniques of visualizing your own secret garden in meditations and for calming the spirit. But this which I was suddenly experiencing *was* the Spirit. The spirit in all of its glory, nothing in between - no deliberate effort, no meditation. It was something which I had finally stopped seeking and trying to explain and had simply surrendered to.

The days passed and this new awareness did not fade. It was as if I had walked through a gate, never to return to the dull colors and predictable life that lie just on the other side of the fence.

Small things remained the small things they are. And as for the "big" things, I found an inner peace which was so large that it existed as my world, with me centered calmly in the middle where I could sense out the reality of the situation.

I could feel the trend in situations and was able to remain serene. I was also able to catch my "old self" in a tendency to look for the point of panic - "what should I be feeling now?" instead of "what am I truly feeling right now?"

My strongest self was able to not only resist, but reject those old tendencies. I was able to choose, or not choose to become stressed by it all.

Furthermore, there was a deeper understanding which was simply present and helped me to realize that creating energetic waves of stress and worry would serve no purpose.

In fact, worry would only contribute to a lesser outcome. I was able to "see" the greater life view and participate in the lighter side of existence…where you walk among embers unscathed, where angels guide you through the forest and lead you into the safe space of your garden.

Most of all, I could see the miracles life offers: You breathe the air and feel the sunshine on your face and drink in what has been placed before you. You see what has always been there.

These are the things which became visible when I quieted my mind, transcended the mere act of looking and began to see.

The mind's incessant chatter can interfere with all aspects of life, but especially in the "seeing" and the understanding of our reality. This chatter must be dropped, over and over again, for it comes back nearly instantaneously.

How Do We "Do" This?

In our libraries and on our bookshelves, we have self-help books available that lead us to freedom from the mind's control from every possible angle:

Books like Eckhart Tolle's, *A New Earth* (Penguin) help guide us in the process of disengaging the ego.

Wayne Dyer's excellent series of books, especially the earlier, *Your Erroneous Zones* and *Pulling Your Own Strings* (Harper Torch), guide us through no-nonsense thoughts on unraveling the mysteries of our self-sabotaging thoughts and help to bring clarity to the logic of releasing negative thoughts.

Louise Hay's book, *You Can Heal Your Life* (Hay House), offers excellent guidance in the areas of healing and health, and examines the ways thoughts from our mind influence the health of our body.

There are multitudes of excellent resources available to guide us. Each author focuses in the specific direction for which he or she has been internally guided to best assist the masses.

It seems my personal guidance has become focused on the moment of choice, the moment where we choose Greatness. Sometimes, however, that incessant mental chatter we have been discussing seems to get in the way of the poise and focus needed to make our best choice.

I propose that we give our ego brain something else to "chew on," so it will release its grip on micro-managing the daily things and let us utilize intuition above thought and stress for the decisions that matter.

I discovered that truly "seeing" provides just such a pacifier. Waking up the senses with the choice of awareness brings new consciousness into your spirit. This consciousness has always been there; it's just that the mind, being very powerful, has become dominant.

What is known as the "left brain" thrives on analytical thinking. For myself, I believe that it was analytical thinking that opened the door to the repetitive thinking world of "shoulds," "what ifs" and worry.

The left brain turns these types of questions over and over in the mind, trying to solve the riddle.

The problem is, in most cases there's not enough information to make a rational decision or opinion.

If you had all of the facts, wouldn't any decision come down to a simple matter of choosing?

But in so many cases, we are faced with variables and unknowns. We try and try to choose a path, but not enough information is available.

At these times, we must be able to "see" clearly enough to understand we are dealing with something where not enough facts are known. At these times, we must be clear and strong enough to be able to switch to right brain thinking and rely on our free flowing intuition to make choices.

The Zen of Seeing

To develop greater ability to experience your free flowing intuition, begin to see your reality for the miracle it is: the young child, the elderly person, the skyline view out your office window, the singing birds and the flowering plant by your door. Fill your senses with this awareness of the world's beauty, for it is life-changing.

Practicing "seeing" the beauty which surrounds you in every direction will keep you engaged in a special kind of free-flow, creative thinking. The left brain will be constantly entertained with creative possibilities.

For me, this practice has allowed my mind to become calm with the recognition we are swimming in a glorious sea of potential and possibility.

We must forever realize there is nothing in this sea which is not connected. Just as if we were bobbing in an ocean...in this "energy ocean" everything touches everything else.

Wiggle your toe and the whole ocean moves. Wiggle your thoughts and the energy also travels outward. Flail about and you lose energy to the sea, sending your energy out and away from you, allowing it to crash on some distant shore.

Choose to stay centered and calm and float in this sea, observe her beauty, weather her storms as they arise, and be rocked by her when she is calm.

PART THREE:

BE

CHOOSING GREATNESS NO MATTER WHERE YOU ARE IN LIFE

Self-Love Is The Root of Choosing Greatness

One idea has repeatedly presented itself to me as I wrote this book: Choosing Greatness is an act of self-love.

Even during the times when I was stuck for just the right words along the way, allowing myself the "sticking" and the blank page led to the conviction that self-love is a most necessary ingredient in choosing Greatness.

To love yourself in all moments, whether you are stuck in a tide pool or flowing with the full force of a raging river, this is the challenge.

Self-love honors your soul, your source, and understands that no matter your physical age, you are like a child learning and making your way through life.

Love, for yourself, for others and for our planet forms the foundation for choosing Greatness.

Flow Like a River

Flow like a river,
around the rocks.
Flow from high mountain ideas,
ever so steadily to the Sea of Prosperity.

-Lynn Alison Trombetta

17. Intention: Be a Better You

"Success seems to be connected with action. Successful people keep moving. They make mistakes, but they never quit."

- Conrad Hilton

Ultimately, it is your choices that add up to who you are and how your life will be. That is, your thoughts, formed into words and actions can become habits that demonstrate your character. It all adds up to who you are, who you might become and how you will live out your days.

You bear responsibility for your choices, but you also have "response-ability." By making the choice to love and trust yourself at your deepest level, your choices and thus responses and actions will align with your deepest desires and will also benefit others along the way.

This is what this book is all about: How, through choice, to Be a better You!

Be Love

The only real "Doing" for you to accomplish is to make the choice to love and trust yourself and to be happy, right now!

Does the idea to simply "choose" happiness sound too easy?

Remember if you allow it, your mind will create negative thoughts and throw them like bricks onto your path in an effort to slow you down. You don't need to know why this happens; you simply need to understand that it may. As they used to say in the 1970's – "Just keep on truckin'!"

Everything good distills down to love. Be love, love yourself, and choose happiness along the way.

Be a Healthy Mind

Mental-emotional self-care is a choice. You learn to see yourself from a different viewpoint and are able to make decisions about how you are choosing to run your life.

Meditation is a key ingredient in this kind of introspection. Often, people get hung up on what they believe the experience of meditation should feel like and this can become a block to experiencing what meditation actually is: a quieting of the mind.

It is that simple. Although meditation comes in many, many forms, some based in religious or spiritual ceremonies, at its root, meditation is simply the quieting of the rampage of thoughts which occupies your mind.

Meditation habits can be chosen and added into your day, developing a slowing down into a practice which strengthens you and guides you throughout your life.

In Part Four of this book I offer several brief meditations for you to experiment with. Whether you choose to practice in silence or with music, indoors or outdoors, please choose to add some form of contemplation or meditation to your daily routine. It will strengthen you in unanticipated ways.

I would also like to mention here the importance of getting enough exercise. Traditionally, the brain has been thought of as a completely formed organ which we use to think with until, through aging, we begin to lose some of its function.

This much feared decline may include the loss of mental sharpness and thinking ability as well as memory loss.

There is however, new hope. Recently scientific studies have drawn the conclusion that the brain needs exercise as much as the body for retaining and even expanding its capabilities. It makes perfect sense to realize that the increase in oxygen intake that exercise produces would also benefit the brain with increased blood flow, so be sure to include exercise in your plans for a healthy mind. As always, before you begin, check with your medical practitioner regarding any health issues or concerns.

Taking time for yourself to calm your mind is truly an act of self-love. At first, the changes will be subtle, but as your energy changes, you will notice the positive effect it can have on your life.

Be a Healthy Body

To have a healthy body, you must realize that choosing positive thinking is essential. Thoughts then become the currency you trade for a healthier outcome. The connection between the mind and the body cannot be over-emphasized here.

Replacing negative, self-defeating thoughts with healthy, positive thoughts is a choice. It is *the* choice, whether we are speaking about health, happiness, or outcomes in general.

From the positive vantage point this offers, choices for what best foods to eat, when and how to get enough rest, and ways you will keep your body active and in motion become nearly effortless. There is plenty of good information available to aid you in your quest for a healthier body.

You learn that each time you choose what is best for you, you demonstrate self-love.

Be Action

Realizing your greatest dreams requires you to complete the circle of bringing thought from nothing to something. Remember that your choices add up to who you are and how your life will be through your thoughts formed into words and actions.

The "action" you must utilize is to choose Greatness at every opportunity as you complete the circle of bringing thought from "nothing" to "something" to change your world.

Stay active in efforts that align with your greatest dreams. After all, you are not just manifesting the situations and things that you desire; you are manifesting your world…your reality.

18. Be Oneness and "Be Here Now"

When my younger son, Jason was only five he said, "Mom, I can't stop thinking about everything around me. I look at something, like a tree, and I wonder, 'What's inside of that?' and I imagine it. Then I think, 'And what's inside of THAT?', and I imagine more. And it keeps going, I imagine smaller and smaller, deeper and deeper inside of the tree. But it seems that it goes forever, getting smaller and smaller, and I'm pretty sure it never ends."

He was fully present in the moment as he pondered his personal reality.

Much has been written on the idea "be here now," the simple concept of being present with your thoughts. Pause, look around and you will suddenly realize you have stepped out of your head, your mind, and into your reality.

This awareness will intensify as you simply observe the world around you: Trees aren't just trunks with leaves; leaves aren't only one shade of green. There are textures and color variances all around. And, as Jason said, "I'm pretty sure it never ends."

The sky isn't only blue; it may be rich reds, golden yellows, intense violets and deep aquamarine. The lake reflects the clouds, the ocean wave glides along the sandy shore with a lacey foam edge.

Become aware and you are suddenly present, in this moment. Notice everything, and all of the mind's talk will be left behind on the surface as you delve deeper into the place the present moment naturally holds.

Planet Earth's gift to the casual observer is her amazing beauty. This beauty is so stunning and breathtaking it at once grabs the attention, jarring us out of complacency and away from our minds talk and pulls us in to the incredible nuances, from the great to the small.

The trailhead is there, where you pause. The path is easy, laid before you, a journey you began by simply opening your eyes and truly seeing.

Use your moments in Nature for such observation and then keep this method ever present. For what the natural world has shown you here, exists everywhere, and is endlessly "One." The path is glistening with love and miraculous things to see every step of the way, every moment of the day.

Just be here now.

19. Be a Part of a Better World

The gift of any contemplative practice, whether it is meditation, prayer, or simple contemplation, is a transformation of the heart. Such practice creates the quiet mind where the seeds of hope grow for a better tomorrow toward the good of all.

Through the receiving of this "gift," you will see more clearly the many ways you may create suffering in your own mind and in the lives of yourself and others. You will also discover much clarity in the ways you may create harmony and cultivate the connection of Oneness and love.

With the intention of creating a better world for all, through practices of contemplation you learn you can actually choose how to "be" in the world. You have opportunities to recognize and change the habits of your mind that create suffering. You have the chance to discover and choose new thoughts and develop new habits to create more happiness for yourself and others.

More than ever before, our world needs this kind of consciousness, this kind of change.

Thoughts chosen for the good of all, together with the thousands of actions which will accompany this intention for every man and woman truly have within the seeds of transformative Greatness!

This "One" word says it all.

I like to believe the concept of Oneness has grown, nearly to the tipping point. A vast population can now see the connection between man and his environment and how we affect ourselves and every other person on the planet with our actions toward the land, the water, and the air.

Earth is a living, breathing planet. We humans were granted the gift of consciousness and thought. Focused on ourselves through time, we ran like carefree children and were not always respectful of our home, our families and our neighbors.

However, we are wiser now, and we are learning how to see truth with our eyes, understand truth with our minds and feel truth with our hearts.

In this truth, we are One with other living beings, with the waters, the land, and air. We are One with our planet, our home.

Above all, we know in our hearts that each of us has the power within to become the "one" that can make a difference.

Are you the river? Are you the One?

PART FOUR

TOOLS

FOR CHANGE

Throughout *Choosing Greatness to Change Your Life*, I have used the idea of a river of energy and intention that flows through us at all times. That "river" is the essence of who we "are" at our very core.

Sometimes, we seem to know little about ourselves and are surprised at our own behavior…our river takes an unexpected turn, changing direction or flowing more powerfully than expected. Alternatively, occasionally the river's energy level drops and it is all one can do to keep moving.

The challenge for choosing Greatness is to begin to know your "self." Know the ways you might slip in choosing the best option, action or behavior. Learn through introspection to spot the pitfalls and choose another path along your journey. Develop your Greatness Muscle to live by your true nature at all levels at every opportunity.

Here are some tools for practice that will help you to discover and rediscover your inner best, your Greatest You!

EXERCISE: MANIFESTING YOUR DESIRES

When you think about manifesting, does your imagination dance with wonderful thoughts of material things and situations you would like to create in your life? It certainly seems that through the practice of meditating you could develop your manifesting skills.

However, your energy is likely to be scattered and your efforts may fall short if you lack a clear understanding of the process that is at work.

Your thoughts are the seeds that create your tomorrows. But a mere thought does not necessarily contain the quality of energy required to bring about change in your life. Water the seed of thought with emotion, or passion and strong feelings!

Here is where the magic begins: as you water that seed with strong emotions, your thought changes from "thought" into "experience." You will be engaged in what it "feels" like to realize your desire.

This is when visualization comes into play: You visualize the desired outcome AND experience the strong feelings that being, doing or having the outcome or object brings. This changes your energy one step closer to manifesting what you desire.

Observe how you respond to your own feelings as you experience this change. Apply a high degree of attention to your thoughts. Stay in alignment with the change and realize that you are actively engaged in the process toward realizing your dreams.

To see how your thoughts might be affecting your ability to manifest your desires, try this easy exercise:

Fold a piece of paper in half lengthwise and, pen in hand, sit comfortably and relax. Try to recall a time when you were able to realize a dream of yours most effortlessly.

Using the first thought that comes into your mind, at the

top of one side of the paper write a brief description of about the dream you realized. Keep it simple.

Now, think back and score yourself 0 to 5 on each of the following five important ingredients for manifesting, with 5 being the highest score:

Visualizing: How clearly were you able to imagine what you wanted?

0   1   2   3   4   5

Intention: How strong and focused was your desire and your intention?

0   1   2   3   4   5

Expectation: How great was your expectation for success?

0   1   2   3   4   5

Alignment: How well did your daily behavior and choices match your intention and desire?

0   1   2   3   4   5

Trust: How strong was your trust in the universe to produce the desired result?

0   1   2   3   4   5

ADD FOR TOTAL: _____

Next, as comparison, think of something you have been wishing for, but that has not yet manifested for you. Use the other column of the paper to write a brief description.

Do the exercise again.

How do your scores on each side of the page compare? In the second set of answers, can you spot which areas scored lowest, indicating less strength? Which of the five areas need more consideration for manifesting?

Are you able to visualize your desired outcome? Do your choices align with your wishes and intentions?

Realize that small adjustments in your thinking can have

a big impact on your results. Have fun with this as you learn to observe yourself in the process and discover how your thoughts, emotions and your intentions assist in fulfilling your greatest desires.

Exercise: Getting in Touch with Your True Self First

Communication is such a huge component of our lives, yet we often are engaged in it without much forethought. The obvious communication these days comes in the form of cell phones, the internet and various electronic mediums.

Other forms of communication, such as verbal discussions and personal interactions include body language that is noted by your brain at a subconscious level. That is, your mind will pick up clues from the other person's body language during the conversation. Without some conscious attention to these clues, you may misunderstand the other person's meaning and end up in reactive communication without knowing why.

Now, more than ever, you need a way to balance yourself. This will assure that you are representing your true self, from a clear place deep inside, when you interact in the many ways that can occur during your day.

One of the best ways to become solid about who you are and how you would like to present yourself to the world is through meditation. Introspection and gratitude are important first steps toward healthy communication in all relationships.

Getting in touch with your dominating thoughts about yourself as you "tune in" to understanding who you really are, at your core, sets the stage for greater communication with others.

The easy meditations that follow approach the idea of introspection from two different angles. If you choose, try the one that most appeals to you first. Then, feel free to experiment with the other.

Method One: Quiet Your Mind

With a very active mind, this technique may prove the more challenging, but the rewards when you quiet your thoughts and attain an "empty mind" are profound.

It is best to develop a habit of daily meditation, preferably in a safe, quiet space that you can return to each time.

Meditating after doing yoga is helpful, as the focus of your mind on the postures and exercises of yoga tends to help you to let go of everyday stresses that may have been dominating your mind. From the post-yoga state, you may find greater success with any meditation.

- To begin, sit comfortably.
- Take a deep cleansing breath, in through the nose and release the air out through your mouth.
- Relax.
- Focus on your breathing and then switch your attention to notice what is happening with your thoughts. As thoughts enter your mind, release them. More will come.
- Go on releasing until the chatter quiets down and your mind becomes still. If more thoughts come in, just go on releasing. Give yourself permission to "empty out." Stay with this technique for three or four minutes.

As the mind calms you will begin to enjoy a great sense of peace. More practice will create greater "emptiness" and even greater peace. The cumulative effect over time is a strengthening of your connection to the quiet power that resides inside of you. This will translate to a more solid foundation from where you will understand the connection we all share and be able to communicate your thoughts, wishes and dreams with others.

Method Two: Observing Yourself (as mentioned in Chapter Two)

This meditation technique is a good way to develop awareness of what you may be communicating to others through your actions and body language.

This simple technique requires only that you stop and mindfully observe yourself at infrequent intervals throughout the day. The effect will be as if you were to randomly pass in front of a mirror or a storefront window and catch a glimpse of yourself.

- How are you carrying yourself? What does your stride communicate - do you seem confident or downtrodden?

- Next, notice what your thoughts are at this very moment of observation. Is your quality of thinking more negative than positive? Is this quality reflected in your posture? Do you notice tension being stored in your body? Does the tension show in the way you stand, the look on your face?

Being suddenly mindful can "turn on the lights" for you. When you realize the strong connection between your thoughts and your body, it is easy to recognize that the random uncontrolled chatter inside your mind may be sabotaging not only your thinking, but your communication with the world around you as well.

When you acknowledge this, it becomes much easier to shift your thinking into a higher place and lift your entire being up into a greater experience of life.

The simple act of taking a moment of awareness to notice your "self" is all it takes to begin.

Exercise: Imaginary Ruler

You tried this one in an earlier chapter. I have repeated it here for your convenience:

When it comes to happiness, where do you find yourself now? Try this easy exercise:

• Hold an Imaginary Ruler in your hands and pretend the left side of the ruler represents disappointment and discontent, and the right side of the ruler represents extreme happiness and contentment with your life.

• Where along this imaginary scale do your feelings fall? Now, try this:

• Close your eyes and remember a time or place when you felt great happiness in the moment. Hold on to the feeling in your mind and experience all you can within the memory. Simply remember every sensory perception you can from that moment.

• Was the warmth of the sun on your face? Were you alone, or with someone you loved? Were there fragrances or smells in the air? Was there a breeze? Were you smiling? Are you smiling now, as you call up the experience in your mind?

Recalling the high points, the "touch points" of your life when you have felt connected to the full, moment-to-moment experience of being alive can be a valuable tool for increasing your present moment happiness.

These high points and recalled moments carry a "soul charge." Focusing on such positive experiences with gratitude will recharge your battery and put you easily in touch with your true self.

Try the Imaginary Ruler experience again.

• Close your eyes and reconnect with your "touch point" for a moment.

• Visualize the ruler once more.

Where along the ruler's edge are you now? Were you able to move your happiness quotient up the scale by recalling times of joy?

Stay in touch with yourself. How are you feeling now? Is the light of your soul connection shining through?

Inherently, as souls, we are each connected to all that is. It is the recognition of this connection that deepens our spiritual relationship with life and intensifies the quality of our daily experience of loving life, loving others and loving ourselves.

As previously discussed, simply being in touch with the *feelings* generated by your thoughts is a big first step in turning up the happiness in your life.

These feelings are the very place where happiness begins!

Exercise: The Art of Improvising for a More Creative Life

What is improvisation? Improvisation is spontaneous and creative energy that springs from relying on your own creativity and the magic of your mind to combine existing ideas and insights into new expressions of yourself.

By freeing yourself from self-imposed "rules" about the way things "should be done," you become more adept at spotting new opportunities and creating the kind of life you want to live.

We all share the ability for improvisation with musicians and artists and other creative spirits. This "gift" lives inside of us just waiting for us to become aware and tap into the greatness therein.

Whether your interest is art, music, gardening, parenting, or any one of a million other things, allowing your creative spirit to participate is most gratifying. This will give birth to ideas and spontaneous creations that draw inspiration from every experience that came before.

Here are a few ideas to spark your improvisational self:

• Combine two ideas to create something fresh and new.

• Play with the edges of your usual thinking and ask "what if?"

• Try new things and allow yourself creative input in the way things are done.

• Take a different route when you walk or on your way home. New scenery, new encounters all add up to creative input for your improvisational mind to work with!

Nature Meditation: Awakening Spring Meditation

Bring the sense of spring's fresh new life and growing qualities into your consciousness with this meditation.

Spring awakens in you, just as it does across the earth. The spring equinox is the time of new life and new growth. You can sense it long before it arrives and anticipate what surprises will fill the gardens and our hearts.

The meditation below will help you to bring that sense of fresh new life into your consciousness with the energy spring brings for growth and change.

Try this meditation either outdoors in nature or near a window in a comfortable place where the temperature is neither too cool, nor too warm. You may wish to have a pen and small notepad or journal at your side to record any thoughts as you complete the meditation.

• Take a deep cleansing breath as you begin; then relax your breathing.

• As your breath slows, look around and become more aware of your surroundings. There is a world of difference between "looking" and "seeing." Today, you will "see."

• Observe nature speaking to you. Allow any remaining stress or thinking to slip away.

• With your focused attention, notice something with each of your senses: The scent of the air, the plants and scenery, the sounds of birds singing, the breeze in the trees. Feel the warmth of the sun on your face, the earth at your side.

• Reflect quietly on the passing of winter and the rebirth of spring that is beginning. What signs reveal this change?

• Continue to breathe in the beauty of this energy.

• This is a time for growth. Close your eyes. Visualize spring and give relaxed thought to qualities you would like to grow for yourself this spring: wisdom, radiance, patience, compassion, understanding, and love.

- Imagine these qualities coming into full bloom in your life. Feel the warming emotion that more of each of these qualities would bring to your daily life and to those around you.
- Now, close your eyes and sit silently for a few minutes.
- Imagine you can ask Nature to give you a message about your personal growth during this time of the year. Stay quiet as you pay attention to any images, words, sensations, impressions, symbols or any form of message you receive.
- Stay quiet and savor this moment of peaceful spring awakening for as long as you wish. Be immersed in this experience and absorb it into your being. As you experience the renewal of springtime, radiate vitality outward.
- When you are ready, open your eyes and become present in this place and time. If you wish, write in your notebook or journal.

Allow the vitality of spring renewal to remain with you as you go about your day.

NATURE MEDITATION TO HONOR MOTHER EARTH

Every year we celebrate Earth Day and its environmental focus. This meditation is filled with love to honor and bless our beautiful planet year round.

•   Begin seated in a comfortable position with your eyes closed. As you breathe regularly, allow your mind to settle into the quiet space you have chosen.

•   Observe your breathing and begin to see how with each breath you are connected to the planet's air, water, soil and inhabitants.

Feel this connection to Earth through the ground.

Imagine this connection through the air you share with other living things.

Visualize how the water in our bodies is a part of the water that covers the planet.

•   Pause and allow this feeling of interconnectedness to expand, larger and larger. Allow it to grow within until it is so large that you find yourself "inside" of the feeling.

•   Recognize this feeling as love. Fully experience this feeling in your heart as you visualize and bless Earth. Vow to treat her with respect and care for her as a loved one.

•   Grow the feeling larger and expand it outward as you imagine that it spreads across the planet, ascends above the clouds and descends deep into the earth. Feel it resonate within you until you are no longer separate from it and you have become the feeling.

•   Slowly, return your attention to the place where you are seated.

•   Carry this feeling of expanded love and connection with you throughout your day.

Meditations for Connecting

"To love someone is to see a miracle invisible to others."

-Francois Mauriac

A Loving Meditation for Caregivers ~ "I Love You Just the Way You Are"

Caregiving can stress even the best relationship, whether it is with our child or other loved one. Chronic, ongoing stress and fatigue can make it difficult to feel love for others and oneself.

This gentle meditation will extend a loving message to your child, another, or the child within to help see the good and the possibilities for happiness that are tucked away inside.

•   Sit comfortably and take a few deep breaths as you allow your body to relax. Bring awareness to your heart. Imagine warmth and relaxation in this area.

•   Now, imagine the other person's smiling face.

•   Feel love as you allow your heart to open and connect to the energy of the other's heart.

•   Relax gently into this. There is no hurry here, only peace and a gentle place to allow loving energy to flow between you.

•   Love is an energy that permeates life. Allow yourself this moment of surrender.

•   From here, send the following loving messages to the other with the intent and understanding that the messages are meant for both you and the other:

"I love you just as you are."

"Thinking of you, I smile."

"You are so precious."

"I love you."

"You are beautiful in my eyes."

"I am grateful that you are in my life."

"My heart is open to great possibilities for you and the things you CAN do."

• Take another deep breath. Acknowledge that the true nature of your relationship is love. Love is the energy you share. Give and receive love from this meditative state where anything is possible.

• Slowly return your focus to your physical surroundings. Carry this centered state and the feelings of peace and love with you. Pause to refresh the feelings as often as you can.

"FROM A DISTANCE" MEDITATION

To cultivate tolerance, inner peace and stillness, try the meditation below.

- Sit comfortably. With a few deep breaths, release any tension in your body and allow your mind to come to rest on any situation with which you are having difficulty.

- Imagine that you are able to "zoom out" the focus on the situation and on anyone involved.

- Relax until you imagine that you are viewing the scene from a distance and that you can no longer hear any harsh words that may be spoken.

- Watch this scene in your mind.

- Offer blessings and allow understanding to pour in: Each person wants to be heard. Each wants to be understood and accepted.

- Send love from your heart to the scene as you watch and imagine that the energies intertwine.

MEDITATION FOR INNER PEACE AND VITALITY

Invest a few moments to fortify what you have to offer your loved ones and the world. Try this easy meditation to calm your mind and body, enhance your intuition and create a haven of inner peace.

• In a quiet place, away from interruptions, sit comfortably. Rest your hands on your thighs, close your eyes and begin to relax. Breathe deeply, sensing the slowing rhythm of your breath. As the relaxation washes over you, smile.

• As you exhale, imagine any stress, anxiety or sadness leaving you. As you draw in your next breath, imagine happiness filling every cell of your body. You can experience this as a sensation of comfort, coolness, warmth, as a fragrance, or as a lovely color flooding into your being. Continue for at least five minutes. Bask in the beautiful, peaceful, centered space you have created.

• Take a deep breath, open your eyes, and sit quietly for a moment to re-enter your world.

• Throughout the day, take occasional deep breaths to reconnect to the experience.

Meditation Experience:

Slow Down and Take Your Thoughts for a Walk!

Just as focusing on your breath can provide a meditative experience, so too can focusing on your steps as you walk. The "left, right, left, right, left, right" of walking can lay out a clean canvas from where a colorful meditation can be born.

The meditation described below will allow you to enjoy Nature while you develop clarity and perspective on your life. Plan to do this once a week: Think of it as "taking your thoughts for a walk" as you allow your brain to unwind and let go of usual thought patterns, as you invite fresh ideas in.

• **Choose**: Choose when and where you will take your thoughts. Think of this as time away from your usual thinking patterns and let go of any thoughts. Early morning, with the day ahead of you, is a good choice.

• **Prepare:** Clear any restrictions on your time so that you can go where your feet want to take you. Wear comfortable clothing and walking shoes. Pack a water bottle and take a walking stick if you are going to walk on uneven terrain. Remember to take your cell phone in case of any emergency; just silence the ringer during your walk.

• **Go:** Slip out your door and go to a place of natural beauty. Anticipate the luxury of time in Nature while you leave your work and stresses behind. If possible, stay on marked trails or walking paths so you do not have to focus on your destination.

• **Enjoy:** Walk aimlessly without rushing. Enjoy the views, the sights of others and the activity of Nature. Truly feel the pattern of walking and notice as your feet touch the ground. Listen for the sounds of life around you. Reverberate with Nature, relax into it and allow your mind to be free. Allow any thoughts that enter to dance through like butterflies on the wind, releasing them to fly away. If your mind catches on a thought, just remind yourself that this is a moment of personal freedom, and release it.

• **Finish:** Keep going until you feel you are finished, then turn around and enjoy the walk back. As you return, notice if any predominant thought of clarity occurs to you. Do not force it; just allow it to bubble up like fresh spring water in your mind. Carry your refreshed perspective with you throughout the week!

Sensory Input Meditation: The Scent of the Land

As Helen Keller once said, "Smell is a potent wizard that transports you across thousands of miles and all the years you have lived."

The memories of smells can produce longing unlike any other as you link them to an experience from the past.

You could easily take your senses for granted as you go about your life. Yet, the sense of smell goes on recording sensory input. You are likely not aware of the depth within the mind where the sensory experience is scribed, that is, until a memory arises to transport your thoughts to another place and time.

Take a hike or a walk with the intention to give yourself a little gift in a present moment that will surface much later, perhaps when your body has grown too old to hike the raw earth and sit motionless with eyelids closed under a favorite mountain tree.

Find a lovely spot in Nature and create that memory now.

Create it without creating it; just let it come to you, without trying to shape the experience, without trying to receive a particular message.

Relax and softly focus on your breath and your beating heart. Draw in the air, close your eyes and simply receive.

Clear your mind and allow the impressions of scent and sound to fill your awareness and create a keepsake, a scented, sonic "touchpoint" of "now."

Just sit, smell the scent of the land, and receive. When you are finished, open your eyes and see with fresh, new awareness.

Special Tips:

Thoughts on Music, Meditation and Mindfulness

As a musician, I notice the many qualities that music and meditation share. Mindfulness is a key ingredient in both practices. Through mindfulness, you can get to a place beneath the clutter, chatter and judgments that can suppress your creative mind.

In an interview about his music and his meditation, jazz legend Herbie Hancock was quoted as saying, "The cool thing is that jazz is really a wonderful example of the great characteristics of Buddhism and great characteristics of the human spirit. Because in jazz we share, we listen to each other, we respect each other, we are creating in the moment. At our best we are non-judgmental."

Anyone who has experienced music from the inside as a musician will understand. When you are mindful with your singing or performing on a musical instrument, you are not thinking about what you will have for dinner or anything other than the music.

Anyone who has experienced meditation will also understand this place of deep focus, non-judgement and bliss.

Meditation is called a "practice" for a reason; as with music, you must practice. With repetition, the process becomes easier and floats you away into a river of tranquility with the waters to recharge and reset your mind for the way you will conduct yourself with mindfulness in daily life.

This skill of mindfulness assists with your day, as you have greater control of random thoughts and emotions and are able to recognize them as separate from your own creative mind. You become skilled at taking a step back from what you might view as reality to see things from a more holistic point of view.

From a centered place rediscovered in meditation, you will develop the quality of mindfulness to which Hancock referred.

Like jazz music, life is improvisational, and with mindfulness, you create as you go.

If you are not meditating regularly, here are some tips to inspire you to include this practice in your life:

- Try to set aside a special time for meditation that can become a routine for you. Whether it is daily or a few times a week, a consistent routine will give you more consistent results.
- Choose a quiet place where you will not be disturbed during your meditation.
- If desired, put on some music to begin your focus and quiet your mind. (See Tips for Choosing Music for Meditation)
- Release any expectations about how your meditation "should" be and allow thoughts to flow naturally until your mind settles into quiet and peace.

CHOOSING MUSIC FOR MEDITATION

Selecting music for meditation requires some forethought for best results. Here are tips to guide you down the right path. Experiment with different genres of music to discover what works best for you. Try online samples based on the category descriptions below to zero in on meditation sounds you will love!

Acoustic Instrumental Music: This is music performed with instruments such as flute, guitar, and piano, without lyrics or singing, and generally without synthesized music tracks. Whether consisting of simple or more complex melodies, the purity of the instruments rings true and the sounds will resonate especially well with a mind during meditation. (Visit MeadowlarkMusic.com to hear samples from some of my CD releases.)

Nature Sounds Added: Instrumental music may have glorious sounds from nature interwoven into the recording. Some artists rely more heavily on sounds such as birds and waterfalls while others use these natural sounds sparingly as "seasoning" to the composition and performance. Either way, Nature sounds can add to the journey as you are soothed and relax into your meditation.

Soft Vocals Added: Just the right touch of vocals in this type of music can be set to words, or be a series of tones sung in heavenly harmonies that weave throughout the main melody. Think "angel voices" adding softness and sensations of soaring to your meditation.

Synthesized Instrumental Music: This type of music can be smooth and flowing or textural and repetitive with strong rhythmic patterns to engage your mind. Just the right synthesized music can create textures and soundscapes to draw you deeper into your meditation.

If you have had difficulty with slowing down into your meditation, repeated rhythmic patterns can help to engage the brain and draw the focus away from everyday thoughts, allowing you to relax into the sounds. In some recordings "looping" Nature sounds or vocals are added.

Pay attention to which genres from the list above seemed to appeal to you. As you begin your search for new meditation music, look for instrumentation that will impart a joyful spirit. This includes wind chimes, flutes, singing crystal bowls, harp, oboe, and solo piano as well as anything else that appeals to your senses.

You will find music CDs suitable for meditation in the New Age and even classical genre sections as well as in those areas categorized for meditation. For a refreshing and relaxing classical approach, enjoy the all-time favorite, "Spring" from Vivaldi's "Four Seasons."

Special Help for Parents and Children:

The Guardian's Creed
by Lynn Alison Trombetta

I promise to stay awake and in the moment. I vow to look through new eyes each day and to transcend what society and even my own parents have taught me about the way the world works and discover anew for myself. After all, these are changing times.

I promise to tend the garden of the world's children, nurturing, protecting and guiding. I choose Greatness in all things for them. I choose never to put a toy gun into a tiny hand or plant seeds of violence with electronic games that confuse a child's reality.

I promise to stay in consciousness, and limit as much as is possible the information that gets "in" and becomes a part of their reality and strive to balance those things I might judge as "bad" or harmful that he or she may encounter with lessons of love and guidance to help him or her navigate our changing world.

I promise to stay alert in times of strife and to know the children who are close to me well enough, through my awakened observation, to see when there has been a change in behavior or personality.

I promise not to keep a family member's or friend's mental illness (or even my own) as a secret that cannot be discussed with those truly capable of showing loving concern within my family; and as a community member I promise to help watch over, not judge, and help ask for and find solutions for those in need.

The Wizard of Oz - A Good Family Film to Share

One of my favorite films, *The Wizard of Oz* (1939) is full of spiritual lessons and ideas with which to identify!

The year 2019 marks the 80th Anniversary of the release of the film. While truly groundbreaking in its technique, it also has enabled generations of audience to derive from the story their own, individual spiritual meaning.

As you strive for choosing Greatness, this film offers it all: lessons of the heart and illusions of the mind; lessons about personal values and self-worth; lessons of fear and of courage, and lessons of gratitude for the gift of a loving family and home, no matter the imperfections.

This would be a good time to reflect on the wisdom contained within this classic. From which character or characters can you most identify with and learn?

Are you like the cowardly lion, filled with unreasonable fear over even the smallest of things? Can you gather strength and become courageous? Alternatively, are you a bit rusty on matters of the heart, like the tin man? Are you like Dorothy, searching outside of herself for her happiness? Are you unable to see your own value like the scarecrow?

We so often seek happiness outside of ourselves and wander our own yellow brick road, but all paths lead home – to who we are "inside." This journey traverses a lifetime, but through our spiritual selves, we can see "the way."

Ultimately, we come to understand that "the way" is love.

When we operate our lives from a loving attitude, with the good for all in mind as we travel that road, our heart shines brightly and returns such goodness tenfold.

This favorite quote by L. Frank Baum, the author of the book that led to the magnificent movie says it well:

"A heart is not judged by how much you love;
but by how much you are loved by others."

I leave you with these final thoughts in the form of a little story I wrote that places the power of creating a world that you love solidly in your own hands; like shifting sands longing to be sculpted, day by day throughout your lifetime.

CONVERSATION WITH AN ENLIGHTENED CHILD

A woman walking her small dog along the shoreline encountered a young child playing in the sand. The woman commented, "Oh, what a beautiful day!"

The child smiled up at her, "Yes, I made it myself!"

"You made it yourself?"

"Yes," the child answered. "Well, that is, everything I needed was here when I got here, but I put things the way I like them."

The woman was intrigued, "Interesting. You did a nice job."

"Thanks. I just finished. You can move things around and change it a little for yourself if you want."

"You wouldn't mind?" asked the woman.

The child continued patting the sand, "No, not if you keep it all nice."

The woman watched the child a moment more and then asked, "Would you be interested in helping me with that?"

The child replied, "I already did. It's your turn now."

Lynn

ABOUT LYNN ALISON TROMBETTA

Lynn Alison Trombetta is an American author whose love of nature is evident in *Choosing Greatness to Change Your Life* as well as in her whimsical adult fiction. She writes to reconnect with the magic of true spirit for a joyful, limitless life based on personal creative evolution and awareness.

Other works by Trombetta include two novellas, *Pie in the Skye* and *Wounded Birds* and *I Go to the Ocean and Talk to Myself*, a book for youths of all ages that she wrote and color illustrated.

Trombetta is also a visual artist, professional flutist and recording artist with the group Meadowlark. A freelance writer on topics of nature, creativity and wellness, she lives in Sedona, Arizona with her husband, guitarist, Rick Cyge.

Visit www.LynnTrombetta.com for more information.

www.ChoosingGreatness.com

OTHER WORKS BY LYNN ALISON TROMBETTA

BOOKS

Pie in the Skye... a fantastic journey through the landscape of your imagination into the knowing of your heart!

Wounded Birds … "Pigeons, and Gators and Ants! Oh my!" A light-hearted fantasy novella and a bit of a mystery that brings the five women who live together in 1980's Phoenix, Arizona new insights and strength.

I Go to the Ocean and Talk to Myself … a colorful book for youths of all ages that delivers the message that what you say to yourself every day has the power to create how your life will be. Written and illustrated by Lynn Alison Trombetta.

Visit www.LynnTrombetta.com

MEADOWLARK CD'S AND DIGITAL MUSIC

Original and Celtic music performed by Lynn Alison Trombetta on flute and Irish whistles in the Meadowlark ensemble with guitarist, Rick Cyge and studio contributions on violin, mandolin, light world percussion and more.

First Light ~ Celtic and original music inspired by Nature

Legend of the Land ~ Visually evocative originals inspired by Nature and the desert southwest

FreeFall ~ Joyful, celebratory original music

Tranquility ~ Relaxing original music inspired by Nature for inspiration, contemplation and massage

A Silent Night ~ A beautifully unique collection of Celtic favorites and traditional Christmas music.

Visit www.MeadowlarkMusic.com

153

Use the following blank pages
for notes to yourself.